GLASNOST, PERESTROIKA, AND THE SOCIALIST COMMUNITY

Glasnost, Perestroika, and the Socialist Community

Edited by
Charles Bukowski
and
J. Richard Walsh

PRAEGER

New York
Westport, Connecticut
London

Library of Congress Cataloging-in-Publication Data

Glasnost, perestroika, and the socialist community / edited by Charles
  Bukowski and J. Richard Walsh.
      p. cm.
    Includes bibliographical references.
    ISBN 0-275-93130-7 (alk. paper)
      1. Communist countries—Politics and government.   2. Glasnost.
  3. Perestroĭka.   I. Bukowski, Charles J.   II. Walsh, J. Richard,
  1954-   .
  D850.G53   1990
  947.085′4—dc20   89-23050

Copyright © 1990 by Charles Bukowski and J. Richard Walsh

All rights reserved. No portion of this book may be
reproduced, by any process or technique, without the
express written consent of the publisher.

Library of Congress Catalog Card Number: 89-23050
ISBN: 0-275-93130-7

First published in 1990

Praeger Publishers, One Madison Avenue, New York, NY 10010
An imprint of Greenwood Publishing Group, Inc.

Printed in the United States of America

The paper used in this book complies with the
Permanent Paper Standard issued by the National
Information Standards Organization (Z39.48-1984).

10 9 8 7 6 5 4 3 2 1

For Jeanie
C.J.B.

For Susan
J.R.W.

Contents

Introduction ix

Chapter 1
Poland and Czechoslovakia: Test Cases for Perestroika 1
David S. Mason

Chapter 2
Developing Socialism in the Soviet Union and China 41
J. Richard Walsh

Chapter 3
Cuba: Guarding the Revolution 63
Juan M. del Aguila

Chapter 4
The Impacts of "Restructuring" and "New Thinking" on Soviet-Vietnamese Relations 87
Daniel S. Papp

Chapter 5
Glasnost and Afghanistan: The Mirage in the Desert 109
Stephen Blank

Chapter 6
Gorbachev and the Korean Issue 129
Roy U.T. Kim

Chapter 7
Conclusion: Assessing the Impact of Glasnost and Perestroika   151
Charles Bukowski

Selected Bibliography   165

Index   171

About the Editors and Contributors   175

Introduction

The extraordinary changes that have been taking place in the Soviet Union since Gorbachev's ascent to power have not lacked in receiving attention in the West. Gorbachev's efforts to encourage openness in most areas of the Soviet system, and his attempts to restructure the Soviet bureaucracy, generally referred to as glasnost and perestroika, respectively, are potentially the most significant changes to take place in the Soviet Union since Lenin's time. The importance of these changes has not gone unnoticed by the Western community of scholars. Indeed, the amount of literature being written on glasnost and perestroika is nearly overwhelming, and the crush of material has been compounded by the abundance of information coming from the Soviets themselves. One Soviet scholar writes of "piles of file folders containing six-month-old newspaper clippings marked 'urgent' or 'critical' that have now been buried by more recent 'priority' articles."[1]

The heightened degree of interest being paid to the Soviet Union is unquestionably commendable. The changes taking place in the Soviet Union under Gorbachev are historic. The acquisition of a better understanding of these changes is a fundamental responsibility of the scholarly community. However, the bulk of the attention from this community is focused on what Gorbachev's reforms mean for the future of the Soviet political, economic, and social systems. Relatively little attention has been paid to how glasnost, perestroika, and related programs might impact on socialism outside the Soviet Union. As the predominate socialist state in the world, events taking place in the Soviet Union are likely to have an impact on other states that claim a socialist orientation. In some cases, the impact might be intentional and direct, part of a conscious policy adopted by the Soviet Union. In other cases, the impact may be indirect and even unintentional, given the complex and interdependent nature of world politics and economics. Such cases represent additional risks facing the Soviet Union as part of its efforts at reform.

This volume seeks to make a preliminary assessment of the impact of glasnost, perestroika, and related Soviet reforms on selected socialist countries. Since the socialist community today has become so diverse, it would be beyond the scope of a single volume to examine the ramifications for other socialist states of Soviet reform in all its aspects. We have chosen to examine a sampling of socialist countries that is roughly representative of the types of socialist states in existence today.

Since we anticipated that the impact of Gorbachev's reforms are likely to be quite diverse, we permitted chapter contributors to approach their topics in whatever manner they felt was most appropriate—singling out areas where the impact is likely to be strongest. While this decision may distract somewhat from the unifying nature of the volume, we feel that it avoids forcing the contributors to look for impacts that might be marginal or not exist at all. In addition, such an approach allows the contributors to work with their strengths. The balance between unity of purpose and depth of knowledge is always difficult to maintain in an edited volume such as this. We hope that the reader finds the balance we have selected to be an appropriate one for this topic.

We also would like to address our use of the term "socialist community" in regard to the title of this volume. By strict definitional standards, it is a misnomer to call the nations that aspire or adhere to socialism a "community." Given what we know today of the history of the socialist world, one may legitimately question whether there ever was a socialist community in the sense of a group of nations espousing a socialist ideology, pursuing similar goals, and undertaking extensive cooperation with one another. Tito's break with Stalin in 1948 initially calls this concept into question. Certainly the Sino-Soviet rift left no question that there was not a single socialist community. Today the diversity of states that call themselves socialist leads many to wonder whether it is possible even to arrive at a common definition of a socialist state.[2]

Yet the term socialist community often has been used to identify the socialist states of the world. Our choice of this term seeks the more common usage—a convenient way to refer to all the world's socialist states. We trust that this does not confuse the reader.

Finally, we would like to express our appreciation for the support we have received from our respective institutions, the Institute of International Studies at Bradley University and the Department of Political Science at Wittenberg University. We would also like to thank Hazel Beadles and Jeanne Clayton for secretarial support and our families for their patience, understanding, and support.

Charles Bukowski
J. Richard Walsh

NOTES

1. Harley Balzer, "Can We Survive Glasnost?" *AAASS Newsletter*, January 1989, p. 1.

2. See, for example, Stephen White, "What Is a Communist System?" *Studies in Comparative Communism*, Winter 1983: 247-263.

*GLASNOST, PERESTROIKA,
AND THE
SOCIALIST COMMUNITY*

CHAPTER 1

Poland and Czechoslovakia: Test Cases for Perestroika

DAVID S. MASON

The changes occurring in the communist world are breathtaking and already exceed what most people, even most experts, would have thought possible just one or two years ago. In the Soviet Union, most political prisoners have been released; Andrei Sakharov, who was in internal exile for seven years, has been elected to the national legislature; independent organizations are mushrooming; the press is among the most interesting in Europe; and the Estonian legislature passed a law (subsequently rejected by the USSR Supreme Soviet) that asserted the republic's right to reject Soviet legislation. In Eastern Europe, we see the Polish regime sanctioning the reemergence of Solidarity and providing for openly contested parliamentary elections; the Hungarian regime moving toward the establishment of opposition political parties; the "fall" of governments in both Poland and Yugoslavia; and a proliferation of independent organizations and political protest in almost every country in the region.

These transformations are significant enough to bring into question the very ideology of communism; indeed, in many of these countries, even Marx has been subjected to a searching reevaluation. As each of the communist party states charges off on its own "path," the movement (if it can still be referred to in that way) becomes increasingly heterogeneous and pluralist. The "communist" regimes become more and more unlike each other, and some of them become almost indistinguishable from socialist governments in the West or from left-leaning authoritarian regimes in the Third World.

The impact of these changes is most dramatic and most important in Eastern Europe. Since World War II, this region has been of key strategic and economic importance for the Soviet Union and, as such, a critical battleground of the Cold War. It is also an area in which the potential for democratic politics has been the greatest in the communist world and has, therefore, been a locus of dramatic conflict between liberal and conservative forces, both internally and internationally. In the past, however, the Soviet Union has always stood behind the status quo in Eastern Europe, and has provided powerful backing for the opponents of liberalizing change inside each of these countries.

Now that calculus has begun to change, with the Gorbachev leadership now acting as a major impetus for change in Eastern Europe. The Soviet reforms provide a model for similar changes in the region and give a boost to the advocates of reform in those countries. The conservatives can no longer count on the Kremlin as a potential trump card and, in fact, find themselves and their Soviet counterparts as the brunt of official criticism for acting as obstacles to change.

For the Kremlin, change in Eastern Europe is considered important for a number of reasons. In an effort to stimulate their own economy, the Soviets would like to be able to rely more on the countries of Eastern Europe as a more reliable source of quality goods, and as a market for Soviet products. The region has also been an important source of reform ideas and experiments for the Soviet Union, so some of Gorbachev's efforts can be tested in Eastern Europe and, if they work there, help legitimate the Soviet reforms. Liberalizing change in the region can also help defuse some of the simmering tensions in those countries, and create regimes that are considered more legitimate in the eyes of their own populations. Gorbachev and his associates have enough problems of their own in trying to reorient Soviet society, without having to worry about strikes or protests in Warsaw or Prague. Paradoxically, of course, some of these Soviet goals may work at cross purposes, since the pressure to reform may foster expectations that cannot quickly be met or unleash tensions that cannot easily be controlled, thus jeopardizing the very stability the leaders hope to maintain.

While these issues are pertinent to all of the European bloc countries, they are perhaps most acute and most evident in Poland and Czechoslovakia, though for different reasons. Poland is in many respects already the most liberal country in the region, but after the crushing of Solidarity in December 1981 it was a society mired in stalemate and apathy. The Jaruzelski regime claims to be committed to thoroughgoing reform, but such change has been blocked by a party bureaucracy that was apprehensive about the possibility of another 1980-81. In the past, the conservatives in Poland have had a favorable hearing in Moscow. Now, however, Gorbachev seems to be encouraging the reformers, and the Kremlin is now tolerating changes that could well have been cause for military intervention in the Brezhnev years. The internal political changes in Poland portend a radical transformation of the politics of that country, and could pose as a model for such change elsewhere in the bloc.

In Czechoslovakia, the issue is a bit different. Since the broken reforms of the Prague Spring in 1968, it has been the most conservative and repressive regime in Eastern Europe. Here also Gorbachev has pressured the regime to adopt reforms, and the Kremlin was instrumental in moving long-time party leader Gustav Husak out of power in 1987. His replacement, Milos Jakes, however, has also been a reluctant reformer. There is another major issue here, however, and that is the legacy of the Prague Spring and the Brezhnev Doctrine. The Gorbachev reforms in the Soviet Union strikingly resemble the Czechoslovak reforms of 1967-68. So for the Czechoslovak leadership to endorse those reforms would be to undermine the legitimacy of a regime that has for 20 years rejected and refuted the 1968 reforms.

There is an important issue here too for the Kremlin, which has never repudiated the Brezhnev Doctrine, used to justify the Soviet intervention in Czechoslovakia in August 1968. For the reforms to proceed apace in Czechoslovakia, the Soviets will have to address this issue, but to do so would further undermine the current leadership in Prague. Furthermore, such a reassessment will affect the entire Soviet bloc, and indeed the whole communist world.

Having sketched the parameters of the issue, we will look at these questions in more detail. First, we will review the record of the Soviet reforms, which provide a context for what is happening in Eastern Europe, and examine the Soviet interest and involvement in reforms in the bloc. We will then investigate in more detail the nature and extent of reforms in Poland and Czechoslovakia, and conclude with a discussion of the implications of these changes for Eastern Europe.

GLASNOST AND PERESTROIKA IN THE SOVIET UNION

The impetus for reform in the Soviet Union came from a number of directions, but the factor of fundamental importance was the economic one. Gorbachev's economic reforms are meant to revitalize a stagnant Soviet economy that has been growing at only about 2 percent annually for a decade. The reasons for the slowdown are partly internal and structural, and partly external. The early years of rapid economic and industrial growth in the USSR had been possible because of abundant and accessible natural resources (particularly of energy); a growing and relatively moveable work force; the capacity of the regime to mobilize resources, including human ones, by force if necessary; and a concentration on quantitative rather than qualitative goals. All of these factors began to wither away in the 1970s as cheap resources disappeared, the population became more stable, and the post-Stalinist regimes became increasingly disinclined or unable to use Stalinist means of mobilization. These internal economic problems were compounded in the 1980s by a sharp decline in world petroleum prices and a consequent drop in Soviet export earnings, 80 percent of which are derived from the sale of energy raw materials.[1] In addition, the military burden on the Soviet economy, which had always been high, posed an even greater strain in the 1980s as the Reagan administration fired up military research, procurement, and spending in the United States. Western estimates hold that Soviet defense spending is at about the same level as U.S. spending (about $300 billion annually), but since the Soviet economy is only about half the size of the U.S., the same level of absolute spending consumes twice as much of the economy on a percentage basis: about 12.5 percent of the Soviet GNP compared to 6.6 percent in the United States.[2] Thus the Kremlin had a compelling economic reason for easing East-West relations and slowing the arms race.

All of these factors have had a deleterious effect on living standards in the country. Even the official press now discusses this. A recent article in *Moskovskiye Novosti* (*Moscow News*) asserts that the Soviet Union now ranks between 50th and 60th of the world's countries in per capita consumption of goods and services, and that the share of government expenditures going to human needs is higher in the United States than in the Soviet Union![3] These assertions are more pessimistic even than most Western estimates of the state of the Soviet economy.

The dismal state of the economy provided the underlying need for the reforms, but the spark of initiative came from the advent of a new and younger leadership under Gorbachev and a Soviet elite that had become increasingly educated, critical, and assertive.[4] Gorbachev is now saying what both Western observers and domestic critics have been saying for years: that the legitimacy of the Soviet regime (and other communist regimes) is increasingly dependent on economic success and consumer satisfaction; that economic success can no longer be based on "extensive" growth and the policies of forced industrialization; that an "intensive" pattern of growth requires commitment, hard work, and support from the population; and that such commitment will only come from a public that has some voice and input into the process. As Gorbachev himself has put it, "a house can be put in order only by a person who feels he is the owner."[5]

The result is a series of increasingly radical reform proposals issuing from the Soviet leadership. In the early period of his leadership, Gorbachev talked mostly of the need for "acceleration" (*uskorienie*) of the economy. From the summer of 1986, however, his speeches became increasingly radical, changing the focus to "restructuring" (perestroika) rather than acceleration, and eventually equating restructuring with "radical reform" and even "revolution."[6] Openness and public airing of issues (glasnost) and "democratization" have increasingly been seen as necessary concomitants of economic restructuring and were the centerpiece of the reform proposals at the January 1987 Plenum of the Communist Party of the Soviet Union's (CPSU) Central Committee (CC).

Under the economic reforms, the scope of central planning will be reduced by consolidating central ministries and restricting them to long-term and strategic planning.[7] Under a new Law on State Enterprises, industrial and agricultural enterprises will be phased into a system of economic accountability, "self-financing," and autonomy that will eventually allow them to establish their own prices and production schedules and conclude their own contracts with suppliers and distributors. It will also allow unprofitable companies to go bankrupt, a prospect made real and visible for the first time in 1987 when the government announced the bankruptcy of a state farm.[8] The reform also calls for the introduction of "socialist self-management" into state enterprises, where workers will elect their managers and foremen. Other legislation will allow some measure of private enterprise, permitting individuals to provide services such as repairs and private lessons.

All of these elements of the Soviet effort at reform have been tried out, sometimes under criticism by Moscow, in one or more of the East European countries. The "two-tiered" planning bureaucracy is similar in form to that in East Germany. The enterprise system of self-financing, accountability, and autonomy is similar in both content and nomenclature to the (so far unsuccessful) economic reform program in Poland. The provisions for bankruptcy follow on the new bankruptcy law in Hungary. Workplace election of managers was first implemented in Yugoslavia, where it was for a long time criticized by the Soviets as being revisionist, and then became a major element of "renewal" in Solidarity's Poland. At that time, the self-management issue was a particularly difficult and delicate one, since it was traditionally the party that selected factory managers, through the system of nomenklatura (the practice of restricting certain leadership positions to party members or party-approved people). Workers' elections of managers undermined nomenklatura and threatened the role of the party, and was one of the factors that led to the martial law crackdown in December 1981. Given this dubious record of self-management in Eastern Europe, this aspect of the Soviet reform program does indeed seem "radical."

Gorbachev has increasingly linked perestroika with glasnost, which is usually translated as "openness" but is closer in meaning to "publicity." This policy serves a number of purposes for the Soviet leadership: it helps identify problems that need correction; it serves to build popular support for the regime, particularly among intellectuals; it reduces the population's dependence on foreign and unofficial sources of information (i.e., Radio Liberty and samizdat [underground publishing]); and it helps to dislodge vested interests and shake up the bureaucracy, which the Soviet leadership identifies as being an obstacle to perestroika and democratization.[9] Tsar Nicholas I once complained: "I don't rule Russia; ten thousand clerks rule Russia."[10] A century and a half later Gorbachev must feel the same way. In his speech to the January 1987 CC Plenum, he said "there can be no person beyond criticism or people with no right to criticize."[11] He encouraged criticism of lower level officials, at least, though the stakes were raised somewhat two months later when Viktor Afanasyev, the editor in chief of *Pravda*, told Soviet journalists that even regional and republic level officials, and central government ministers, should also be available targets.[12]

The intellectual justification for glasnost was enunciated by Tatyana Zaslavskaya, the economist who has advocated extensive economic reforms: "if we continue to keep from the people information about the conditions under which they live . . . , we cannot expect them to assume a more active role in economic or in political life. People will trust and support you only if you trust them."[13] The result of this encouragement has been a broadening and deepening of Soviet news coverage, and an accessibility of information, unlike anything since the 1920s. Previously taboo subjects are now receiving coverage. Such issues include joblessness, drug abuse, prostitution, urban blight, catastrophes (such as earthquakes and plane crashes), hijackings, homelessness, youth gangs, homosexuality, and traffic deaths. Even Chernobyl, which was initially hushed up, has since then been addressed in over 460 articles in the press.[14] The director of Glavlit, the main government censorship bureau, says that the list of information that can not be published has been shortened by one-third. According to him, "anything that is not prohibited is permitted."[15]

Perhaps the most dramatic changes are evident in historiography and culture. Stalin, Bukharin, and Trotsky are all being given a more thorough and honest treatment than heretofore, and Bukharin has been officially redeemed. Pasternak has been rehabilitated, *Dr. Zhivago* is finally being published, as is Anatoly Rybakov's *Children of the Arbat*, and some of Nabokov's works will appear in print for the first time since he left the country in 1919. Apparently feeling more confident about the regime's legitimacy and the credibility of the Soviet media, the Soviets in 1987 ceased jamming the Russian-language broadcasts of both Voice of America and the BBC.

The campaign for glasnost is accompanied by an appeal for "democratization" of the Soviet Union. Soviet leaders and writers admit now that there is "not enough democracy" in the country, and Gorbachev has called for a series of political reforms to reinforce the economic ones. The most striking of these proposals is for competitive elections and secret ballots in both the party (up to the union republic level) and the state. In 1987 there were some multicandidate elections in the party at the *raikom* (regional) level and soviet elections with several candidates were held on an experimental basis in 5 percent of the country's electoral districts. The March 1989 elections for the newly created Congress of the People's Deputies also provided for multicandidate elections. Soviet citizens exercised choice with a vengeance, rejecting 34 regional party secretaries, a Politburo member, and a host of other party luminaries, some of whom ran unopposed.

The Gorbachev leadership has sanctioned, and even encouraged, the emergence of relatively independent groups and associations.

Over 30,000 grass roots voluntary associations have emerged, to promote various types of civic improvement.[16] Some of these, such as the "national fronts" established in the Baltic republics, have gone much farther than Moscow would like, calling for greater republican autonomy. Gorbachev has even made overtures to the church. In a meeting with the top hierarchy of the Russian Orthodox Church in April 1988, Gorbachev called for a more tolerant attitude toward religion in the interest of national unity.[17]

The Supreme Soviet has voted to permit popular referendums on regional political and social issues and to let citizens appeal to the courts decisions made by Communist Party officials.[18] There has also been some reduction in the role of nomenklatura. Gorbachev has said that the promotion of nonparty people to leading positions is "an important aspect of the democratization of public life."[19] An important and symbolic confirmation of this principle came with the election of Elem Klimov, not a party member, as head of the Cinematographers Union. As noted above, employees' election of factory managers will also cut away at nomenklatura.

The regime has also eased up somewhat on political dissidents, releasing most political prisoners, allowing Andrei Sakharov to return to Moscow, and even allowing him to visit the United States. Some of the newly released prisoners are testing the limits of glasnost by seeking official permission to publish an independent journal of news and opinions called *Glasnost*. Even more startling has been the relatively tolerant treatment of public protest demonstrations, including those in Khazakhstan protesting the replacement of the Kazakh party leader with a Russian, the public demonstrations of the unofficial nationalist organization "Pamyat," the demonstrations in Red Square by Crimean Tatars demanding a meeting with a Politburo member (which they got); and the enormous demonstrations and strikes in Armenia and Azerbaijan over the disputed Karabakh territory.

All of this is changing the face of the Soviet system, and moving the country increasingly to a "civil society." There are numerous skeptics who wonder "whether real reform is viable at all in the Soviet Union"[20] or who doubt that Gorbachev can win the "race with time."[21] But it is becoming increasingly clear that Gorbachev's intentions are serious, that the reforms are real and not cosmetic, and that, in the short run at least, the changes are far-reaching and significant. There is obviously opposition to the reforms, both in the leadership and in the bureaucracy, but more and more of the central leadership positions are filled with Gorbachev's people, and the major reformers (e.g., Zaslavskaya, Aganbegyan) have been given more visibility and more influence. The question is no longer whether the reforms are real, but whether the regime can carry them through to completion and, even more importantly, manage the destabilizing consequences. Gorbachev himself recognizes the challenge. At the June 1987 CC Plenum, he said that the reforms were "aimed at achieving a qualitatively new level of Socialist society. History has not left us much time to face this task."[22] Even if he succeeds, though, the planned changes will unleash grievances and conflicts that the Soviet system is not well equipped to handle. Jacek Kuron, the Polish dissident, describes the situation as a genie being let out of the bottle: "Gorbachev has set the social forces in motion, and neither he nor anyone else can know what the consequences will be."[23] These "social forces" will be at least as disruptive within Eastern Europe as they will in the Soviet Union.

The Kremlin has already witnessed the potential for fragmentation and instability within Soviet borders, in Central Asia, in the Caucasus, and most recently in the Baltic republics. In October 1988 the Soviet Union's party theoretical journal, *Kommunist*, published an article calling for the "economic sovereignty" of the country's constituent republics.[24] In a classic case of going further than the Kremlin intended, the Estonian legislature the next month adopted an amendment to the Estonian constitution asserting the right of the republic to suspend or limit the application of USSR legislation within Estonia. This was an astonishing display of pluck and independence, and *Pravda* dryly noted that these acts were at variance with provisions of the USSR constitution now in effect.[25] Shortly thereafter the USSR Supreme Soviet nullified the Estonian amendments. This sort of feistiness was exercised within Soviet boundaries; it suggests the even greater challenges the Kremlin might expect from the governments of Eastern Europe.

"NEW THINKING" IN SOVIET FOREIGN POLICY

The changes occurring in the Soviet Union extend into foreign policy as well. Here, too, the basis of the changes is economic: if Moscow wants to develop an economy that is more efficient and more oriented toward consumer goods, it needs to expand trade, attract technology, reduce military spending, and cut back on aid (whether economic or military) to other countries. All of this requires a more relaxed international atmosphere and, in particular, an improved relationship with the United States.

This has resulted in a sweeping reorientation of Soviet foreign policy, both in speech and in actions. The ideological basis for the changes was provided by Academician Yevgeniy Primakov in a major article in *Pravda*.[26] He emphasized the "organic link between our country's domestic policy and its foreign policy," and pointed out that the "radical qualitative change" in the country affected domestic and foreign policy alike. The Soviet Union is now emphasizing political, rather than military, means of insuring its security. Military doctrine should be reoriented to be primarily defensive, and based on "reasonable sufficiency" rather than superiority. Throughout the article, he stressed global interdependence, and the importance of global rather than bilateral issues confronting the world. Foreign Minister Eduard Shevardnadze has made the same point, saying that "the struggle between the two opposing systems is no longer the defining tendency of the present era." What is decisive, he said, was international cooperation "to restore and protect the resources necessary for the survival of humanity."[27]

These words have been matched by a host of Soviet actions to reduce armaments and military spending, negotiate arms control agreements, and cut back on Soviet military commitments in Eastern Europe and the Third World. The official press has often linked the military reorientation to the economic imperative, pointing out that defense spending and the arms race with the West "is one of the basic reasons for the grave condition of the Soviet economy and the slow growth in the people's standard of living."[28] In December 1988 Gorbachev told the United Nations General Assembly that Moscow would unilaterally demobilize a half million troops and scrap 10,000 tanks, including some 50,000 troops and 5,000 tanks from Eastern Europe. The next month he told a visiting Western delegation that the Soviets would reduce their military budget by 14.2 percent and cut the production of weapons and military hardware by 19.5 percent.[29]

This lowered strategic and military profile has been accompanied by a reduced level of activity in the Third World. Soviet leaders and writers now concede that socialism may not be the best path for all poor countries, and some have argued that capitalism may even be beneficial for them, at least in the short run. As one academician put it: in the 1970s "we attempted to expand socialism's sphere of influence to various developing countries, countries that, in my opinion, proved totally unprepared to adopt socialism."[30] Soviet leaders contend that they can not afford to support progressive movements all over the world and that they will do so only when resources allow it and it is mutually beneficial. These words have been followed by concrete actions on a number of fronts: Soviet troops are being withdrawn from Afghanistan; Kremlin pressure persuaded Vietnam to announce a withdrawal of its troops from Cambodia; Cuban troops are being pulled out of Angola; and the Soviets have scaled back promises of assistance to Nicaragua and other socialist Third World governments.

SOVIET POLICY TOWARD EASTERN EUROPE[31]

As Soviet policies toward the rest of the world have changed, so too has the Kremlin's orientation toward Eastern Europe, the region of primary economic, strategic, and ideological importance to Moscow. The fact of genuine political and economic reform in the Soviet Union is itself both interesting and important; it is even more remarkable that the Soviets are also encouraging glasnost and reform in Eastern Europe. Gorbachev and the Soviet leadership have admitted that the Stalinist model of economic and political development no longer works in the more complex social and economic environment of contemporary Soviet society. In pushing such reforms in Eastern Europe, the Soviets are also admitting that the Soviet model has not always been appropriate for their East European client states. The Soviets have a number of reasons for fostering reform in Eastern Europe: to revive the faltering economies of the region, upon which the Soviets depend heavily for trade; to insure political stability and enhance the legitimacy of these regimes at a time of disruptive change; to test out some of the Soviet reforms in the East European contexts; and to confirm the ideological legitimacy of the Soviet system and the applicability of that system to other countries—the "universality" of the Soviet model.

The most important stimulus is the economic one. Soviet plans for perestroika are based on a more technologically based economy and envisage rapid growth of investment in new equipment, especially in engineering and electronics. But this is not to be based on imports of

Western technology. Rather, the Soviets hope to accelerate imports of high-quality machinery (and consumer goods) from Eastern Europe.[32] This has been confirmed in recent decisions by the Council for Mutual Economic Assistance (CMEA) to broaden joint scientific and technological cooperation and to pursue a higher concentration of trade within the bloc.[33] The Soviets already conduct over half of their trade with CMEA countries, and this percentage has been increasing in the last few years. So to a large extent the success of the Soviet economic reform depends on increased productivity, and especially of increases in the *quality* of production, in Eastern Europe. Soviet economists have admitted that "the problems of the economic slowdown exist in all socialist countries in one form or another."[34] Indeed, since the early 1970s, economic growth rates have declined sharply in all of the East European states, except the German Democratic Republic (GDR), where the decline is more moderate.[35] The Gorbachev leadership apparently feels that the path to renewed growth and increased quality is through the kinds of decentralizing and market-oriented reforms that the Soviets are themselves pursuing. Exposing the East European economies more directly to international markets, especially Western ones, will also make them more competitive and contribute to qualitative improvements. Thus we see the Soviets allowing, even encouraging, Rumania and Bulgaria to enter the International Monetary Fund and Hungary, Poland, Rumania, and Czechoslovakia joining the General Agreement on Tariffs and Trade (GATT). Both the Soviet Union and the East European states have also become increasingly involved in joint ventures with Western firms.

The relationship between the Soviet Union and Eastern Europe is a symbiotic one: the Soviets hope the East Europeans will follow their model; but they also hope to borrow from the experiences of the more progressive members of the socialist community. Here, too, there has been an evolution in the views expressed by the Soviet leadership. In his 1985 speech to the East European party secretaries for economic affairs, Gorbachev attacked reforms directed at creating market socialism, and criticized especially the negative examples of Yugoslavia and China.[36] But recently he has increasingly expressed interest in reform and innovation elsewhere in the communist world. In his May 1987 speech in Bucharest, before inviting "the fraternal countries" to borrow from the Soviet reforms, he said "we are studying with close interest the experience of our friends and their explorations in the field of the theory and practice of socialist construction, and we are trying to make broad use of everything that suits our conditions."[37] The Soviets have expressed particular interest in Hungary's market-oriented economic reforms and its multicandidate electoral reforms.[38] The new Soviet project to allow joint ventures with Western firms follows earlier experiments in this area by Bulgaria, Czechoslovakia, Hungary, and Poland. In terms of glasnost, the Soviets are now opening up areas for discussion (for example, drug abuse) that have long been treated in the media of other East European countries (especially Yugoslavia, Poland, and Hungary).

The problem for Eastern Europe, even more so than for the Soviet Union, is that economic reforms are likely to be destabilizing, and to undermine the fragile legitimacy of those governments. Any major reforms will take time to lock in and to produce results, and in the meantime, there may well have to be some belt-tightening. But the legitimacy of most of the East European regimes increasingly has come to rest on socioeconomic performance, so economic stagnation may well jeopardize that legitimacy. "Democratization" is meant to remedy this dilemma, by attempting to enlist popular participation in and commitment to the reforms, and to inject a measure of political legitimacy at a time of economic retrenchment.

During their own struggles over reform, the last thing the Soviets need is Solidarity-type disruptions in Eastern Europe. Moscow could try to avoid this either by imposing stricter regimentation and wielding the threat of intervention, or by encouraging autonomy and domestic relaxation. Gorbachev has basically said that the first of these options is no longer valid, so the only alternative has been the latter. At any rate, the Gorbachev-style economic reforms require the support of the population and, in Eastern Europe at least, such support is unlikely to be won without some quid pro quo. A measure of political relaxation seems to be the quid in this case.

As the reform process accelerated within the Soviet Union, so did Soviet encouragement for reform in Eastern Europe. At first, Gorbachev did not call on the East European countries to initiate reforms. But by the time of the January 1987 CC Plenum in Moscow, it was made clear that the problems of reconstruction and democracy affected "not only" the Soviet Union and that many of the considerations at the plenum had a "universal character." The demands for greater democracy, glasnost, freedom of criticism and justice were being heard "in the whole community, from Hanoi to Havana."[39]

Soviet encouragement of reforms in Eastern Europe was made more explicit with Gorbachev's visits to Prague and Bucharest in the spring of 1987. In his speech in Prague, an important document that will be discussed further below, Gorbachev explained and outlined the process of reform in the Soviet Union and gently prodded the Czechoslovaks to study the Soviet experience: "today a reliable yardstick of the seriousness of a ruling communist party is not only its attitude toward its own experience but its attitude toward the experience of friends." He also spoke of "the sharply growing importance of exchanges of experience in socialist construction and its *generalization.*"[40] In May he visited Rumania's Ceausescu, who was much less receptive to the Soviet reform ideas. But here too he talked of drawing on the experiences of others and hoped that "the fraternal countries [could] find something useful for themselves in the creative work that is under way in our country."[41]

The response of the East European regimes to the Gorbachev initiatives has been varied, according to the reform orientations of the leadership and the nature of regime-society relations. In general, however, almost all of the East European regimes have adopted the line that restructuring in the Soviet Union is a welcome development, that an "exchange of experience" between Eastern Europe and the Soviet Union is good, but that the Soviet experience is not to be copied "mechanically" without concern for specific national conditions.[42] There has been a strange kind of role reversal in Soviet-East European relations, with the Soviet Union now pushing for economic reform and democratization, and some of the East European regimes dragging their feet. In the past 40 years, the most dramatic initiatives for change have come from Eastern Europe, not from the Soviet Union. When incentives for change *have* come from Moscow—for example, with Khrushchev's speech to the 20th Party Congress in 1956—the East European responses have outpaced the Soviet.

As Charles Gati has pointed out, the differences in orientation are due in part to the age and tenure of the East European leaders.[43] Until the removal of Hungary's Kadar in May 1988, Gorbachev was far younger than any of his East European colleagues (only Poland's Jaruzelski and Czechoslovakia's new leader Jakes are under 70) and had far less experience as first secretary (three years compared to an average of 19 years among the allied East European leaders). Not only does this give Gorbachev a different ("post-Stalinist") perspective, but it makes it far easier for Gorbachev to criticize past leaders and past failings, since he assumes no responsibility for those mistakes. For most of the East European leaders, to criticize the past is to criticize the present; it is, in fact, self-criticism. This obstacle may be eased away as some of the older party leaders step down. Already this has begun to happen with the recent retirements of Gustav Husak in Czechoslovakia and Janos Kadar in Hungary. Both of those leaders were associated, to a greater or lesser degree, with the repressions of reform following the 1956 and 1968 events. Now that they have been removed, it is somewhat easier to address those controversial and divisive events. This is beginning to happen in Czechoslovakia, as will be discussed below. In Hungary, the new leadership there has begun to reassess the Hungarian revolution as well. A party committee investigating Hungary's postwar history has declared that "what happened in 1956 [was] a popular uprising against an oligarchy which was humiliating the nation."[44] The government has also announced that Imre Nagy, the party leader executed for treason over the 1956 events, would be exhumed from an unmarked grave and reburied.

The changes in the Soviet Union are affecting all of the regimes in Eastern Europe, though in various ways. Hungary, Poland, and East Germany (after the dramatic events of November 1989) display the most substantial movement. Bulgaria and Czechoslovakia have begun their own reform programs, but at a slower pace. Rumania has resisted the pressure to initiate any domestic reforms. The most interesting cases, however, are Poland and Czechoslovakia. In the former, we are witnessing a potentially fundamental transformation of the system, brought about by a combination of pressures from below and from outside. In Czechoslovakia, the issue of the Prague Spring and the Soviet role in Eastern Europe is being broached and reassessed for the first time in 20 years. The combination of dramatic domestic change in Poland and a reorientation of the Soviet relationship with Eastern Europe, via Czechoslovakia, may change the face of communism.

RESTRUCTURING POLAND

Poland is the premier beneficiary of change in the Soviet Union, and is setting the pace for political reform in the communist world. In April 1989, after eight weeks of "round-table" negotiations between Solidarity and the regime, the parties signed an agreement providing for startling and unprecedented changes. Solidarity was legalized; the opposition guaranteed a bloc of seats in the existing parliament; and a second chamber of the legislature would be created and chosen in free and open elections. So for the first time in the communist world, a legal opposition came into being.

Poland has always been an anomaly in the Soviet bloc and since 1981 even more so: a regime that had crushed Solidarity and imposed martial law, yet which tolerated a flourishing underground press and left at large its most outspoken political opponents. Poland also had the freest press in the communist world (with the possible exception of Yugoslavia), thus presenting a kind of benchmark for glasnost in the Soviet bloc. Consequently, the Jaruzelski regime was the most vocal supporter of the Gorbachev reforms in the Soviet Union, which in turn served to legitimize the limited autonomy and liberalization that the Poles had managed to secure, even before the round-table agreements. In a strange twist over time, the Poles had changed from the bête noire of the Soviet bloc under Brezhnev to the favorite sons of Gorbachev.

The Polish press has covered the Soviet reforms more extensively than any of the other East European countries, publishing in full Gorbachev's major speeches and CPSU resolutions. They have developed Polish translations for the three key Soviet terms describing the reforms: *przebudowa* for perestroika, *jawnosc* for glasnost, and *przyspieszenie* for uskorienie. The Polish media have also reported the release of Soviet dissidents like Andrei Sakharov, Anatoly Koryagin and others, the disturbances in Armenia and Azerbaijan, and other previously unmentionable events. At first, this coverage was almost entirely *descriptive*, with little commentary on the events or discussion of how they might affect Poland.

After the January 1987 CPSU Plenum, however, and even more so after the June Plenum, both coverage and commentary increased dramatically. An index of this increased coverage is the number of entries under the category "domestic politics and economics of the USSR" in the Polish monthly periodical index, *Bibliografia Zawartosci i Czasopism*. During 1986 there were usually two or three entries in this category each month. In February 1987, after the January plenum, there were 14, 11 of which addressed change, reform, openness, or restructuring in the Soviet Union.

After the June 1987 CPSU Plenum, coverage became even more

extensive. In the weekly *Polityka*, for example, there were major, often front page, interpretive articles on the June plenum and Soviet reform (subtitled "the greatest changes since the time of NEP [New Economic Policy]"), on the "blank spots" in the history of Polish-Soviet relations, and on the revised historiography of the Stalinist era, and long interviews with Anatoly Rybakov (author of the controversial novel *Children of the Arbat*) and with Polish Foreign Minister Orzechowski (the article entitled "The Polish Style"), which included extensive discourse on Soviet-Polish relations. By January 1988 the number of articles on the Soviet Union was up to 25 per month.

Poland, more than any of the other countries of the region, illustrates the symbiotic nature of the reform process in relations with Moscow. Soviet leaders openly discussed their interest in the Polish reforms, and the Poles capitalized on the Soviet reforms to push ahead with their own. When Polish party leader Jaruzelski met with Gorbachev in Moscow in April 1987, he noted that

the Polish public is following the course of restructuring in the USSR with avid interest and attention and wishes its Soviet comrades success in this historic undertaking, which also provides Poland with an inspiring example of how a policy of socialist renewal is implemented.[45]

Polish officials have described developments in Poland and the Soviet Union as a process of "mutual influencing."[46] The Poles take a certain pride in the fact that the Soviets have studied their reforms, and even adopted some elements of them. An article on the Soviet reforms in *Polityka* mentioned that the new Soviet law on enterprises was based in part on the experience of the socialist countries, including Poland, and that a number of elements of the new Soviet law were based on the Polish law on enterprises: "In Moscow it is no secret that during his recent visit to Warsaw premier Ryzhkov was interested in the details of the Polish economic reform and that Zbigniew Messner [the Polish premier] gave him the text of our law on enterprises."[47]

In a 1987 interview with Western reporters, the first in two years and itself an indication of the new glasnost in Poland, Jaruzelski praised Gorbachev effusively, and said that the Soviet economic reforms make it easier for him to promote radical economic change in Poland. He also said that for the first time in 40 years [!], the Soviet leader was more popular in Poland than the U.S. president.[48]

The Poles have had a decentralizing economic reform on the books since 1982, but have had little success in implementing it, partly due to bureaucratic inertia and partly to conservative opposition. Gorbachev's reforms, and his railings against bureaucratic resistance in the Soviet Union, have the effect of encouraging the reformers and muting their opponents in Poland. It is now much more difficult for conservatives in Poland to argue that the reforms violate communist orthodoxy when the homeland of communist orthodoxy is pursuing the same kinds of reforms. The Soviets on occasion even directly encouraged the liberals in Poland. An article in the Soviet party monthly *Kommunist* on the Polish party congress asserted that "the party . . . cannot arbitrarily, without considering the situation, set tasks which are correct from the point of view of Marxist-Leninist theory, but which are impracticable in the given concrete circumstances."[49]

The Polish regime has taken the Soviets at their word and has professed it is moving ahead with reform on a number of fronts, in terms of the economy, of glasnost, and of democratization. The 1982 economic reform, which provided for enterprise autonomy, self-financing, and self-management (in Polish, "the three s's") has stagnated, with little real progress in any of the three areas. To try to get things moving, in 1986 Jaruzelski announced a "second stage" of the reform, and set up a Commission on Economic Reform to supervise its implementation. While the details of this second stage were slow in forthcoming, Jaruzelski said that the new economic policies would "eliminate" the present "centralistic model that hasn't passed the test of time" and would rely heavily on market mechanisms.[50] Opposition to this second stage was evident at the end of 1986, when a revised version of the plan watered down much of the original. There was a storm of protest, however, including from members of the Commission, and the revised version was withdrawn. Wladyslaw Baka, head of the Polish National Bank, later said "there is no doubt that the process Gorbachev has initiated in the Soviet Union has been a very strong support for the proreform sector in Poland."[51]

Impetus for the reforms was slowed somewhat by the inability of the regime to attain a sufficiently strong endorsement for the reforms in a referendum in November 1987. Nevertheless, the regime initiated a series of scaled-down but sizable price increases in an attempt to rationalize the price structure in 1988. Many of these decisions made sense in strictly economic terms, but ran into the usual political problems in terms of the impact on workers and the standard of living. For example, the government raised procurement prices for agricultural goods by 48 percent, hoping to insure a more plentiful and reliable supply of foodstuffs to the market. The consequence, however, was substantial increases in retail food prices as well, always an explosive issue in Poland.

In the summer of 1988 the government attempted to make real some of the reform provisions by closing down 21 unprofitable enterprises and warning that 140 others were being considered for closure. One of these was the Gdansk shipyards, where Solidarity was born in 1980 and where union activism remains strong. Both of these decisions contributed to the disaffection that led to a new round of strikes in August.

Just as Soviet perestroika has stimulated economic reform in Poland, glasnost in the Soviet Union has fostered jawnosc in Poland. *Dr. Zhivago*, which was finally published in the Soviet Union, was also serialized in Poland and broadcast over the radio. A new daily television news show, factual and without commentary, is so popular that its ratings equal some of the Western-made shows. The anchor of the program was a member of Solidarity. Censorship has been relaxed, and since the amnesty of political prisoners in 1986, the regime has generally stopped jailing those arrested for publishing samizdat. But the more lively official media has made the unofficial media less controversial and less popular: an issue of the most influential underground publication, *Tygodnik Mazowsze*, which sold 100,000 copies in 1983, now sells only 40,000.[52] In line with Soviet practice, the Polish regime ceased jamming Voice of America and Radio Free Europe, apparently feeling the more open press inside Poland would make those stations less attractive.

Polish jawnosc has proceeded far enough to allow public exposure even to opposition figures. In early January 1988 the official weekly *Polityka* published an open letter to Jaruzelski and Walesa from Jerzy Holzer (an historian at Warsaw University who had written a samizdat history of Solidarity) in which he asserted that neither leader could claim the allegiance of a majority of the population and appealed for a meeting between them.[53] In 1988 the official organization PRON began publication of a monthly, entitled *Konfrontacje*, as a forum for dialogue between the party and the opposition. An early issue featured an interview with Bronislaw Geremek, the independent historian and advisor to Lech Walesa.[54] Opposition figure Adam Michnik published several articles in the (still censored) Catholic weekly *Tygodnik Powszechny* in the spring of 1988. Most startling of all, in November 1988, the regime allowed a live televised debate between Lech Walesa and Alfred Miodowicz, the leader of the official trade union alliance. By the time of the round-table negotiations in the spring of 1989, all of these people routinely appeared on Polish television.

Even before the round-table agreements, the Poles had carried out some limited political reforms. A new law on "Public Consultations and Referendums" aimed at "broadening of citizens' direct participation in the exercise of power"[55] presaged by several months the new Soviet law on referendums. The regime set up a new office of civil rights spokesperson, a kind of ombudsman modeled on the Scandinavian practice, who admitted that in her first ten days of office she received 5,000 letters of complaint.[56]

As part of the reassessment of history in both Poland and the Soviet Union and an adjustment of their relationship, the two countries have begun to address the difficult and sensitive issue of their past relations. When Jaruzelski visited Gorbachev in Moscow in April 1987, they agreed to establish a joint commission of historians to look at the "blank spaces" in the history of Soviet-Polish relations. In the words of the Polish cochair, the commission "will help to open closed pages in our history."[57] Most Poles are familiar with these issues, which include the 1920 war between Russia and Poland; the Comintern's dissolution of the Polish Communist Party in 1938; the 1939 Molotov-Ribbentrop Pact, which divided Poland between Germany and the Soviet Union; the Soviet army's failure to support the Warsaw uprising against the Germans in 1944, and the most delicate and inflammatory issue of all: the wartime death or disappearance of some 15,000 captured Polish army officers in Soviet territory.

In 1943 occupying German forces announced the discovery of 4,000 corpses in Katyn Forest near Smolensk and blamed the Soviets for their deaths; the Soviets blamed the Nazis. A Red Cross investigation at the time suggested that the officers had died in 1940, when the area was still under Soviet rule. The noncommunist Polish government in exile supported the Red Cross investigation, leading Stalin to break off relations with that government and begin building up a cadre of Polish communists, who were to take control of Poland at the end of the war. As independent historian Bronislaw Geremek has said, "for Poles, Katyn dug the roots of the present communist system. That is why, if confidence is to be restored between our two peoples, it must be treated."[58] This whole issue is complicated by the fact that Wojciech Jaruzelski spent the war years in the Soviet Union and quickly moved up in the ranks of the Polish army on Soviet soil; he was, in some ways, one of the replacements for the soldiers lost at Katyn. So his own authority and legitimacy are at stake too.

The potentially explosive nature of these issues has caused the joint commission to move slowly, and as of early 1989 there had been no public report on their findings. However, there were hints of a Soviet reassessment of the story. In May 1988 an English-language broadcast by Radio Moscow on the subject said that "a German protocol which has now surfaced suggests Soviet bullets were found in the bodies."[59] This was apparently based on an article in *Literaturnaya Gazieta* (May 11, 1988) that mentioned the German reports but also said that other reports described the bullets as German made.[60] Perhaps encouraged by these stories, the Polish government finally broke ranks on this issue and boldly declared in March 1989 that Soviet forces were responsible for the massacre.

It is not clear what the results might be of this reassessment of the bilateral relationship, so it is understandable why both sides are moving slowly. On the issue of Katyn, for example, many Poles are as much irritated by the Soviet refusal to admit culpability as they are by the historical events themselves. For them, a more forthcoming stance from Moscow might ease some of that bitterness. On the other hand, a Soviet admission of guilt might simply provide fodder for those Poles who argue that the Russians have had it in for the Poles all along.

Despite all the substantial changes in both form and substance in Poland, the economic reforms have had little effect, given the resistance of bureaucrats and conservatives in the regime and a population that remains sullen, pessimistic, and skeptical of any policies originating from the top. This skepticism has increased as the economy continues to deteriorate in the face of the government's promises of improvements. The economy suffered a negative growth rate during 1981-85. It picked up a bit in 1986, with a growth of 4 percent that year, but it dropped back down to 2 percent in 1987, hardly enough to sustain the kind of recovery Poland needs. Production of meat and dairy products in 1987 was actually less than in 1986. Poland's huge hard-currency Western debt continued to grow, from $33.5 billion in 1986 to over $39 billion in early 1988.[61] The government's efforts to rationalize the pricing structure has simply led to inflation (at an annual rate of about 60 percent in 1988), workers' demands for compensating wage increases, and a consequent wage-price spiral that has further lowered the standard of living.

After the regime's crushing of Solidarity at the end of 1981, most Poles turned apolitical and apathetic, reluctant either to support the martial law regime of General Jaruzelski or the underground opposition of Solidarity. Even after the lifting of martial law in 1983, neither the government nor the opposition could muster enough popular support to break the stalemate.[62] As Solidarity leader Wiktor Kulerski put it: "people prefer to wait. The prevailing feelings are those of passivity, reservation and perhaps even tiredness. There is no will to come up with action."[63] People were disillusioned both with Solidarity and with the government and its policies—even with socialism. Public opinion polls in the early 1980s showed most people supporting the ideal, at least, of socialism. By 1987, however, a study of university students found a majority opposed to "the further construction of socialism."[64] Few saw any hope that the current reforms of the system would work.

In 1988 a constellation of circumstances led to yet another round of Poland's periodic protests. Eight years since the founding of Solidarity, there was a new generation of young people in the work force, and some of them felt neither committed to the old organization nor intimidated by the legacy of 1981. Furthermore this time, unlike 1980-81, there was a reforming leadership in the Soviet Union that would not necessarily support the conservatives in Warsaw. Finally, in 1988, as in 1956, 1970, 1976, and 1980, a new round of price hikes angered the workers and led them out into two rounds of protests and strikes, first in the spring and then in August. The strikes of the first round were largely over the economic issue, and petered out after a few weeks, in some locations with wage increases, in others without.

In August the strikes were more serious, and the political demands, including the legalization of Solidarity, more prominent. This time, partially because of the greater openness to political issues in the media, the television and news media gave full coverage to the strikes. On August 31 (the anniversary of the signing of the Gdansk agreements in 1980), Interior Minister Czeslaw Kiszczak met with Solidarity leader Lech Walesa and offered to discuss the legalization of Solidarity if Walesa could persuade the striking workers to return to work.

After some difficulty with strike leaders who feared a sellout, Walesa was able to prevail, and the strikes came to an end.

The next month, Prime Minister Messner and his entire cabinet resigned, having come under increasing criticism, even in the official press, for lack of progress on the economy. This was the first such mass government resignation in the communist world. Politburo member Mieczyslaw Rakowski was named prime minister and made a bid to broaden the government by including prominent noncommunists as ministers. Most, however, were unwilling to participate pending the outcome of the promised round-table negotiations between the government and the opposition. When the new cabinet was finally constituted, it did include three ministers from the noncommunist satellite parties, and one nonparty person; furthermore, Rakowski left two portfolios (including labor minister) open for possible participation by the "constructive opposition."[65] The new Rakowski government also attempted to push the reform process ahead by publishing a consolidation plan that called for dissolving the planning commission and state monopolies, shifting resources from defense and heavy industry to consumer goods, and sharply cutting restrictions and regulations on the operations of private enterprises.[66]

For the rest of the year, though, Solidarity and the government were unable to settle on ground rules for negotiations. Finally after a stormy session of the party's Central Committee in January 1989, in which Jaruzelski threatened to resign if they didn't approve his recommendation, the party approved a resolution calling for "political pluralism" and opening the possibility for including "constructive opposition in the political system" and "opening up the way to creating new trade unions, including Solidarity."[67] This seemed to open a whole new chapter in Poland's postwar history.

This sudden and startling series of moves by the Polish regime suggests an intervention by an outside force in the person of Mikhail Gorbachev. Ever since the banning of Solidarity, the Polish regime had contemptuously referred to Walesa as "a former leader of a former trade union" and had refused to deal with him. In past strike actions, the government had played on the divisions among the workers and the opposition by making judicious use of the carrot and the stick. The sudden approach to Walesa in August, the replacement of the government, and Jaruzelski's power play at the Central Committee in January suggest that there was another player involved. It seems likely that the Kremlin, fed up with the lack of progress in

Poland and the never-ending strikes, suggested a different strategy, perhaps even threatening a change in the Polish leadership if the situation were not resolved. As noted above, the Kremlin has had enough problems of its own in trying to reform, and was plagued at the time of the Polish strikes with challenges from the Baltic republics and the Caucasus. An upheaval in Poland could well have been the straw to break the camel's back of reform in Moscow.

During Poland's difficult spring and summer of 1988, the Soviet leadership made a number of conciliatory gestures and statements that seemed to encourage a similar response by the Jaruzelski regime to the opposition. In July Gorbachev made a three-day visit to Warsaw in advance of the meeting of the Warsaw Treaty Organization there. During his visit, Gorbachev extended an olive branch to the Polish population, and at the same time pressured the Jaruzelski regime to make further progress toward renewal. In his speech to the Sejm (Poland's parliament), the Soviet leader indirectly apologized for Soviet treatment of Polish communists during World War II: "We condemn Stalin's repressions. As is known, they affected many Polish Communists as well. The deportation of Poles from the Western provinces of the USSR was also a violation of socialist legality. This is a part of the tragedy that our country went through."[68] Gorbachev also reemphasized his theme of a new kind of relationship between Moscow and its allies. Our relations, he told the Sejm deputies, "are being freed of elements of paternalism." The joint Soviet-Polish statement at the end of his visit stressed that relations between the two countries are built on "equality, independence, mutual responsibility and responsibility to one's own people, as well as each country's right to resolve questions of its development as a sovereign state." Their mutual relations continue "ruling out claims to knowledge of the highest truth" and provide for "the sovereign right of each country to independently determine the ways and means of constructing socialism [and] the pace of sociopolitical transformation."[69] It was symbolically important that Gorbachev was accompanied by academician Yevgeniy Primakov, who had written the important 1987 essay for *Pravda* on "A New Philosophy of Foreign Policy."

While pledging to leave the Poles alone, Gorbachev also pressured the Polish leadership to accelerate the pace of reform. Although, he said in the Sejm speech, there can be no "mechanical copying" of one party by another, there is a common understanding on the need for "changing over to a new quality of socialism" and "for a renewal of socialist society." In a speech to a group of intellectuals, he emphasized the need for the leadership of a country not to lag behind the desire of its people for change. His meager praise for Jaruzelski led Poles to speculate that Jaruzelski would be replaced at the special party conference scheduled for early 1989.[70] In a press conference in Warsaw academician Primakov even hinted at Soviet approval for the reemergence of Solidarity: "any new structure which would emerge [in Poland] would be considered as an internal problem of this country."[71]

The August strikes in Poland must have frustrated the Kremlin, and the Soviet press gave unusually broad and neutral coverage of the events. While there were some complaints about "the leaders of illegal Solidarity" and outside support for disruption in Poland, in general the Soviet line was that the strikes resulted from failures by the government. When the strikes were finally ended in mid-September, *Izvestia* commented that "the problems that provoked them, particularly the prices and incomes policy of which the public disapproves, remain and continue to feed the tension."[72] The Soviet press commented approvingly on Kiszczak's meetings with "a number of well-known representatives of various public circles to set up a round-table meeting" that would include people of "various political leanings and philosophies." *Pravda* saw this as an effort by the country's leadership "to broaden the platform of national accord."[73] Walesa's name was even mentioned in some reports.

In the days after the conclusion of the strikes, the Soviet press carried a number of articles critical of the Polish leadership. *Izvestia* on September 17 reported the complaint of Alfred Miodowicz, the Polish Politburo member and leader of the official trade union structure, that the government had not heeded the unions as an "early warning system" and simply waited for the issues to be raised by strikes before addressing them. This, he commented, tended to discredit the trade unions. An article in *Sovetskaya Rossiya* was even more blunt, accusing the Polish leadership of mismanaging the economy and suggesting that the government might have to resign. It said that the strikes and the official trade unions' call to replace the government were a healthy sign of increasing democracy.[74] A few days later, Prime Minister Messner and his cabinet resigned.

The Kremlin was particularly attentive to the Polish events, and Gorbachev's extended Warsaw visit also testifies to Moscow's concern over the Polish situation. The display of Soviet interest in the strikes, plus the unusual turnaround in Warsaw's stance toward the opposition, suggests that Gorbachev may have given Jaruzelski an ultimatum: settle the unrest and reach accommodation with the opposition, or step down from the party leadership. The dismissal of the *government* may have been both a compromise and a warning. When the new Jaruzelski-Rakowski configuration was still unable to bring itself to negotiate with Solidarity, perhaps Moscow renewed the pressure. This could account for Jaruzelski's uncharacteristically bold threat to resign if the Central Committee did not resolve to allow the reemergence of Solidarity. At any rate, it is clear that the Kremlin encouraged these conciliatory moves, even if it did not demand them.

The result of these developments was an unprecedented series of round-table negotiations between the government and Solidarity, which lasted for two months and concluded on April 5, 1989, with a path-breaking set of agreements that went farther than the Party's Central Committee had promised in January. Solidarity was reinstated and received air time on radio and television as well as its own national and regional newspapers. The Solidarity-led opposition was guaranteed 35 percent of the seats in the restructured lower house of the Polish parliament, the Sejm. The Polish United Workers' Party (the communist party) received 38 percent of the seats, and its formerly allied parties the rest. For the first time since World War II, a ruling communist party will be in the minority in an East European legislature. Even more far-reaching was the reconstitution of a second legislative chamber, the Senate, for which elections were completely free and open. Not surprisingly, Solidarity won 99 of the 100 Senate seats and will have veto power over legislation passed by the lower house. Lech Walesa was probably not exaggerating when he said at the signing ceremony of this historic pact: "this is the beginning of democracy and a free Poland." There are enormous implications in these changes for Poland and for the rest of the countries in the region.

The changes in Poland are occurring at a pace few people expected. There is still a long way to go before Poland emerges from its extended crisis, but the possibilities now seem greater than ever before, largely because of the presence of Gorbachev. With the emergence of a legal opposition in Poland, we see the beginnings of pluralism, the erosion of the party's monopoly of power, and a major blow to communist authoritarian rule.

CZECHOSLOVAKIA AND THE LEGACY OF THE BREZHNEV DOCTRINE

Czechoslovakia, like Poland, is very important to the Soviet Union both economically and strategically. The Soviet Union is Czechoslovakia's leading trade partner, receiving 45 percent of the country's exports. Czechoslovakia ranks second, behind only the GDR, as one of the Soviet Union's largest trade partners. As the "dagger in the heart of Europe," Czechoslovakia is also important strategically, bordering on both the Soviet Union and West Germany, and Moscow has stationed about 80,000 troops there.

If Poland before 1985 could be considered one of the most liberal countries in the Soviet bloc, Czechoslovakia was one of the most conservative. Ever since the crushing of the Prague Spring in 1968, Czechoslovakia had been mired in rigidity and dogmatism. Through all of the Brezhnev years, the shadow of the Brezhnev Doctrine hung over both Czechoslovakia and the rest of the bloc. This doctrine, at least as it is called in the West, refers to the justification used by Brezhnev and the Soviet leadership for their intervention in Czechoslovakia in August 1968. This asserts that the world socialist movement has priority over individual national sovereignty, and arrogates to the socialist states the right to protect the gains of socialism. As *Pravda* put it in 1968,

every Communist Party is responsible not only to its own people but also to all the socialist countries and to the entire Communist movement.... The sovereignty of individual socialist countries cannot be counterpoised to the interests of world socialism and the world revolutionary movement.[75]

For Czechoslovakia, the issue of the Prague Spring and the Brezhnev Doctrine combines elements of the Solidarity period and the Katyn Forest issue for the Poles. The reforms under way in the Soviet Union closely resemble the Czechoslovak reforms of 20 years ago; and the legitimacy of the Czechoslovak leadership rests in some measure on its rejection and crushing of the remnants of the Prague Spring. Perhaps because of all of this, however, the Kremlin has taken special interest in the current reforms in Czechoslovakia, and has played a role there similar to that in Poland. But resistance to change is even stronger in Czechoslovakia than it is in Poland.[76]

Early in Gorbachev's tenure, Prague's reaction to glasnost and perestroika was cool, at best. Some of Gorbachev's speeches that contained criticism of central planning and bureaucratization were even censored or altered before appearing in the Czechoslovak press. In mid-1985, party leader Husak asserted that "we will not take any of the roads of market-oriented concepts . . . we have had bad experiences with that kind of thing." By the 17th Party Congress in March 1986, however, there had been a change. By then, Husak said "we are not afraid of any reforms . . . we follow what they are doing in the USSR and we look for our own solutions."[77] A relatively radical reform program adopted at the Congress was, according to Prime Minister Strougal, "in its basic features identical with the aims pursued also by the Soviet comrades in their restructuring."[78]

By the beginning of 1987, the regime was touting glasnost and perestroika in Czechoslovakia and the Soviet Union, and the Czechoslovak media had stepped up coverage of the Soviet reform program. There were still divisions within the Czechoslovak leadership, however, and it may have been these problems that delayed by three days Gorbachev's visit to Prague in April of that year. During the visit it was clear, though, that Husak had thrown in his lot with the reformers. Perhaps he had been under pressure to do so from the Kremlin, as the Polish leadership was. His praise for Gorbachev and the Soviet reforms was effusive, more so even than Jaruzelski's:

You have seen how deeply our people respect you, with what sincere approval they accept your innovative ideas and with what sympathy they are following the thoroughgoing reform you are striving to implement. They rightfully see in them a future that points the way ahead for us, too. . . .[79]

There was, however, a basic tension between Husak and Gorbachev. The Czechoslovak leader, more than any others in Eastern Europe, was associated with the past, with the Brezhnev leadership, and with opposition to reform. Husak bore the main responsibility for the "normalization" in the country after 1968. One could not admit positive elements to the Prague Spring without undercutting the legitimacy of the Husak leadership. There were intriguing signs of this tension between Husak and Gorbachev. For example, the entire Czechoslovak delegation left Moscow in the middle of the 70th anniversary celebrations for their own independence day ceremonies in Prague, but did not return for the important November 7 parade.[80] Six weeks later Husak stepped down as party leader, "due to his age" (75) and was replaced by Milos Jakes. The continuing ambivalence of the Czechoslovak leadership toward the Gorbachev reforms was evident already in Jakes' first days, when the party daily *Rude Pravo* mistranslated a crucial word in Gorbachev's congratulatory telegram to Jakes. Gorbachev's reference to "the renewal of socialism in Czechoslovakia" was translated as "a strengthening of socialism." The Russian word for renewal (*obnovlenie*), which Gorbachev often uses, is best translated into *obnova* or *obroda* in Czech and Slovak. These are the terms that were used to identify the reforms of 1968, so the Husak leadership had avoided their use.[81]

Jakes is a moderate in the Czechoslovak leadership: neither the hard-liner Vasil Bilak nor the liberal Lubomir Strougal managed to win the position as Husak's successor. Jakes played no major role in the Prague Spring in 1968, though as chairman of the party's Central Control and Auditing Commission he was in charge of the purges of the reformers in the aftermath of the Soviet intervention. Nevertheless, he is not as heavily burdened with the legacy of these events as was Husak. It would now be somewhat easier for Prague, and Moscow, to reassess that critical year.

Since 1981 Jakes had been a full member of the ruling Presidium, with primary responsibility for the economy, which was the area of primary focus under Prague's own restructuring (*prestavba* in Czech). Within a month of his selection as secretary-general, Jakes made a one-day visit to Moscow, where the two leaders agreed that "the overall direction of restructuring in the Soviet Union and Czechoslovakia is identical."[82] But the new leadership was apparently not comfortable about moving quite as fast as their Moscow colleagues. In an interview with the West German media, Prime Minister Strougal said that they were "attentively following" the reforms in their neighboring countries but that the Czechoslovaks did "not want to compare ourselves with Hungary, the USSR, or Poland; we are much more modest. We do not want to be an international model for the world."[83] This was a revealing disclaimer and suggests that someone (perhaps Gorbachev?) did want them to be such a model. Later, Jakes also expressed reservations about the scope and pace of the reforms in other countries, saying that some of them had "some negative consequences" that the Czechoslovaks had to be wary of.[84]

The Czechoslovak economic reform program was begun under Husak, and has moved ahead under Jakes. The reforms adopted at the 17th Party Congress and reaffirmed in the January 1987 "Principles of Economic Restructuring" called for a "comprehensive experiment" to be carried out for three years and, if successful, to be introduced throughout the economy in 1990. By early 1988 the experiment had been extended to 69 enterprises responsible for about 30 percent of the country's centrally planned industrial production.[85] The reform looks much the same as the Soviet one, with a reduction in central planning, economic accountability for enterprises, and fuller enterprise autonomy. Enterprise managers are given significant control of parts of the budget, the labor force, wages, production programs, investment, and contracts. Pay will vary according to performance and enterprises will be able to export directly, without going through government ministries.[86] A new law on state enterprises, similar to both the Polish and Soviet bills, provides for workplace self-management and elections of directors. A government reorganization will cut the central administrative staff by 30 percent—some 11,500 people.

The government is now admitting that the old economic system "has essentially run out of its capacity for direction and motivation."[87] In the face of these good intentions, however, the reform faces formidable obstacles, as in both Poland and the Soviet Union. As the Soviets discovered in their experiments with the Liberman reforms in the 1960s, it is difficult implementing a reform in only part of the economy, as the Czechoslovaks are now doing. This problem is compounded by the delayed reform of the pricing system; without realistic prices it is difficult to implement cost-accounting, profitability, and so on. There is also the problem of apathy on the part of the workers. Even official surveys show that some 60 percent of the employees in the enterprises under the experiment are passive or apathetic toward the project.[88] Indeed, this is part of a more general phenomenon on apathy and privatism that seems as widespread (and officially recognized) in Czechoslovakia as it is in Poland. Furthermore, as party leader Jakes himself admitted in an interview with *Time* magazine, there is considerable opposition even to the principles of the reform, particularly among those concerned about growing inequality under market conditions.[89]

As in the Soviet Union, intellectuals and political leaders in Czechoslovakia have made the connection between economic reform and glasnost (the Czechs usually use the Russian term), calling for a wide "supply" of information and the presentation of a wider range of views on major issues. An extremely strong case for glasnost was made by Jan Fojtik, a Central Committee secretary, at the 9th Congress of the Czechoslovak Journalists' Union in Prague in 1987. He argued that the media should assure "that the working people are the subject of policy, and not its mere object" and went so far as to argue that "one needs no censorship, nor any sort of 'self-censorship.' . . ."[90]

Obviously censorship has not been eliminated, but the press, even the party press, has opened up a bit for discussion of broader points of view and readers' letters. On the 50th anniversary of the death of Tomas Masaryk, the country's first president, *Rude Pravo* published its first article on him in almost 20 years.[91] There is more openness in films and literature, with publication of works by previously banned authors such as Franz Kafka and Bohumil Hrabal.[92] The government has stopped jamming some Western radio stations, such as the West German Deutsche Welle. The regime no longer attempts to isolate Alexander Dubcek (the party leader during the 1968 Prague Spring) from sympathetic outside contact, and he has consequently conducted several interviews with the Western media. One of the many ironies of the Czechoslovak situation, however, is that the media there offers relatively little coverage of the Soviet Union, where the press is so much more open; but since Soviet television programs are accessible throughout the country, Czechoslovaks can naughtily watch Moscow's broadcasts to find out what is really happening.

In Czechoslovakia there has not been as much movement or progress in "democratization" as in either Poland or the USSR. However, there has been some progress in this area, both in terms of rhetoric and action. There has been discussion of the possibility of secret ballots in party elections and multicandidate elections for the state. The government has eased up on travel restrictions somewhat. In a concession to the increased national consciousness sweeping the country (and the rest of the region), in October 1988 the government sponsored a celebration of the country's 1918 independence, the first time this has been allowed since 1968, when Dubeck had restored it as a national holiday.[93]

The increased official openness and official professions of support for pluralism have encouraged more active unofficial political action as well. There is a boom both in underground publishing and in the formation of independent association. In August 1988, 10,000 people marched through the streets of Prague to mark the 20th anniversary of the Warsaw Pact intervention in that country. It was the largest such demonstration in 19 years and was made up mostly of young people, suggesting the emergence of a new generation of activists. In January 1989 several thousand people marked the anniversary of the death of a student who 20 years earlier had set himself on fire to protest the Soviet intervention. Despite forceful action by the police, the demonstrations continued for five straight days. The country has also seen a dramatic increase in interest in religion and the churches. More than 400,000 Roman Catholics signed a petition for religious rights and freedoms after Cardinal Frantisek Tomasek, who is 88 years old, urged them to do so in a letter from the pulpit. As a result of this pressure from below, combined with pressure on the regime from the Vatican, the Catholic Church in Czechoslovakia was able to consecrate three new bishops in 1988, the first in 15 years.[94]

In Czechoslovakia, the *unofficial* reaction to Gorbachev's reform program has been even more positive than the official one. Jaroslav Sabata of the Charter 77 human rights organization has said that "Gorbachev has opened up a new climate here. He is destroying the old atmosphere of fear."[95] In his interviews with the Western media Dubcek calls for "unconditional" support for Gorbachev's initiatives. He told Austrian television that "what happens in the Soviet Union now is well-suited to our conditions," and he criticized Prague's leadership for being so "very selective when it comes to deciding on what suits Czechoslovakia and what not."[96]

Dubcek and others have pointed out the similarities between what is happening in the Soviet Union now and the attempts at reform in Czechoslovakia in 1968.[97] The issue of the Prague Spring and the Soviet intervention are the most sensitive and difficult ones facing the regime in Prague, and they raise substantial issues about the USSR's past and present role in Eastern Europe. In 1987, 18 former Czechoslovak party members expelled from the party in 1968 wrote a letter to *Rude Pravo*, which did not publish it, pointing out the similarities between their goals in 1968 and what Gorbachev is attempting now.[98] Prague has waffled on the issue, sometimes admitting that the slogans of 1968 "seem to resemble those now used by the CPSU and CPCZ [Communist Party of Czechoslovakia]"[99] and other times claiming that "a profound abyss lies between restructuring in the USSR and the CSSR [Czechoslovak Soviet Socialist Republic] and the intentions of that time."[100] This ambivalence and caution on the part of the leadership in Prague has continued under Jakes.

It is clear, however, that this issue is being debated within the Soviet Union too, and in fact Moscow has moved further toward a reassessment of the Prague Spring than has Prague. This was first hinted at in late 1987 by Georgi Smirnov, an historian closely linked to the leadership, who told Western reporters that it was time for "a new assessment" of the events.[101] About the same time, a Soviet Foreign Ministry spokesperson said that the main difference between the "Moscow Spring" and the "Prague Spring" was "nineteen years."[102]

An even more definitive signal came a few months later, when Leonid Yagodovsky of the Soviet Academy of Sciences told a Japanese communist daily that Brezhnev's crushing of the Czechoslovak reforms had been "absolutely wrong" and "a mistake." He said that a revision of attitudes on the Prague Spring was being prepared by his Institute of the Economics of the World Socialist System. The appointment of Jakes had created the opportunity for a reevaluation "because the reforms pursued in the Soviet Union today are essentially identical with the entirety of the reforms of 1968."[103]

The results of this report, a comparative analysis of the Czechoslovak reforms with the present Soviet reforms, were presented in *Moscow News* in August 1988. The report found that both reforms were based on the same principles. The problem in Czechoslovakia was that the economic reform ran into resistance from conservatives, so radical reform in the social and political structure also became necessary.[104] This is a strikingly different portrayal of the situation, and seems to place the blame on *conservatives* rather than on "antisocialist forces" as the canon had. It does, however, fit into the current Soviet interpretation of the reasons for the slow progress on reform in both the Soviet Union and Czechoslovakia.

The same issue of *Moscow News* contained a round-table discussion of the Prague Spring with Soviet journalists who were there at the time. Every one of them was critical, in one way or another, of the Soviet actions at the time. Several complained, for example, that when Brezhnev came to Prague in February 1968, they wanted to tell him "the situation as it was," but he would not hear them out. Consequently, they said, "sometimes the facts were tailored to fit" orders from above. In drawing "lessons" from those events, the journalists asserted that other nation's problems cannot be solved through military force, and that "in relations among socialist countries, a situation in which one country arrogates unto itself the right to make decisions for others cannot exist."[105]

This kind of language is similar to that used by Gorbachev in describing the new relations among socialist states, although Gorbachev himself has not yet directly addressed the issue of the Brezhnev Doctrine. In fact, when he was asked about that doctrine in his meeting with Polish intellectuals in Warsaw, he simply promised to respond later in writing (though he apparently has not yet done so). It remains a sensitive and highly charged issue. While Gorbachev may want to renounce the Brezhnev Doctrine (and the incidents above suggest he does), to do so entails multiple risks. First, it challenges his own conservative opposition in Moscow, which remains formidable. Second, it risks destabilizing the Prague regime and undercutting Jakes' legitimacy. As Zdenek Mlynar (one of Dubcek's advisors in 1968) has put it: "It's one thing to rehabilitate former leaders like Bukharin, who are long dead. It's something entirely different to rehabilitate figures like Dubcek, who are still among the living and who can make speeches and receive support and express opinions."[106] (This argument is slightly undercut, however, by the apparent rehabilitation of real live figures like Sakharov and Walesa.) Finally, a renunciation of the Brezhnev Doctrine risks further instability in the other East European states. The Brezhnev Doctrine, whether explicitly stated or not, does act as a restraint on revolt or revolution in these countries. The possibility of Soviet intervention may serve to mute more radical voices in Warsaw or Budapest, and encourage the more moderate lines of people like Adam Michnik, who counsel *evolutionary* change. So even if Moscow does not intend to intervene in Eastern Europe, it might be helpful for some people in those countries to think that it might.

CONCLUSION

The changes occurring in the Soviet Union are momentous, and there should no longer be any doubt that they are real and serious. This is not to say that they could not be reversed, but the longer the reforms continue, the more deeply they become entrenched, and the more difficult it will become to reverse the process. If the process does continue, it portends a dramatic transformation of the socialist system in Europe.

Poland and Czechoslovakia are key players in this process. Poland is now emerging as the first "post socialist society"[107] that is increasingly pluralist in its economic, political, and social structure. To the extent that this process continues without a violent upheaval, and if the Kremlin allows the process to continue, Poland may become a model for the evolution of other East European societies, and a consequent "Finlandization" of Eastern Europe. It is in this context that the Czechoslovak case becomes relevant. The Czechs had moved in that direction 20 years ago, but were crushed by Soviet tanks. If the Kremlin is going to allow Poland to follow and pass the precedent of the Prague Spring, it will have to renounce the Brezhnev Doctrine, either explicitly or tacitly. As noted above, there already seems to have been a step back from the doctrine in the Soviet Union, if not in Prague. For the Soviets to loosen the strings on Eastern Europe in this way could pave the way for a very different kind of Europe. This has long been the dream of many intellectuals in Eastern Europe, and the concept of a "central Europe" has reemerged in both West and East, stimulated in part by an article by the émigré Czech writer Milan Kundera.[108]

There are many obstacles to this process, however, and not just from bureaucrats and conservatives; there are other more systemic problems. One of these is the strategic one. While it is conceivable that the Soviets would allow a *neutral* Eastern Europe or central Europe, it is inconceivable that they would tolerate a shift by these states into the Western orbit. This was an issue, in fact, that was raised at the summer 1988 Soviet party conference.[109] So, as with all of Gorbachev's other reforms, the issue is one of limits; how far can things be allowed to go without becoming dangerous or unstable?

Another obstacle is the ideological one. An Hungarian official, for example, has wondered whether if they do not "clarify the matter of principle, if we continue to proceed pragmatically, we will fail to resolve the question of what is socialism and how it is different from Western capitalism."[110] This is not just an abstract issue of interest to ideologists. In fact, most people in Eastern Europe *favor* socialism, or at least those elements of it associated with the provision of benefits such as housing, medical care, employment, and social welfare. Broad support for these principles is affirmed by most prominent dissidents, as well as by public opinion data.[111] Yet the market-oriented reforms threaten to undermine these few remaining attractive features of state socialist societies. This is the reason why Gorbachev has so much difficulty in attracting popular support for his reforms, and the East European leaders will confront the same problem.

An American historian wrote recently that "the interim achievement of the opposition in the Soviet bloc is to have destroyed the moribund form of politics as hitherto practiced there," but they have not talked much about the form that the systems there *should* take.[112] While this is true, it errs in assigning exclusive credit to the opposition. The process has been a long and symbiotic one in which the opposition and the leadership affect each other. The political leaders in Eastern Europe are, for the most part, quite different than those of ten years ago. In particular, they have had to learn how to deal with an opposition that is increasingly sophisticated. This has caused the party leaders themselves to be more sophisticated and, in the process, *politics* has emerged in Eastern Europe. It is still not clear how all of this will come out, and what form these societies will take. The regimes do not know and the opposition does not know. But as both sides debate these issues, between and among themselves, the debate itself means the system is already changing.

NOTES

Research for this chapter was conducted in part while the author was a visiting scholar at the Hoover Institution, Stanford, California, and supported by funds provided by the U.S. Department of State through Title VIII of the Soviet-East Europe Research and Training Act of 1983.

1. Axel Lebahn, "Political and Economic Effects of Perestroika on the Soviet Union and Its Relations to Eastern Europe and the West," *Aussenpolitik* 39, no. 2 (1988): 107.

2. *World Military Expenditures and Arms Transfers, 1987* (Washington, D.C.: U.S. Arms Control and Disarmament Agency, 1988), p. 12.

3. *Moskovskiye Novosti*, August 21, 1988, p. 12; translated in *Current Digest of the Soviet Press* (hereafter *CDSP*), October 26, 1988, p. 27.

4. For a discussion of this point, see Gail W. Lapidus, "Gorbachev and the Reform of the Soviet System," *Daedalus* 116 (Spring 1987): 6 and 16.

5. *Pravda*, January 28, 1987; cited in Werner Hahn, "Electoral Choice in the Soviet Bloc," *Problems of Communism* 36 (March-April 1987): 29.

6. *Pravda*, August 2, 1986; see discussion in Lapidus, "Gorbachev and the Reform," p. 11.

7. See Alice Gorlin, "The Soviet Economy," *Current History* 85 (October 1986): 325 ff; and Paul Hofheinz, "Gorbachev's Double Burden: Economic

Reform and Growth Acceleration," *Millennium: Journal of International Studies* 16 (Spring 1987): 21-31.

8. *The Wall Street Journal*, March 27, 1987, p. 11.

9. For useful discussions of glasnost, see Lapidus, "Gorbachev and the Reform"; Archie Brown, "Gorbachev and Reform of the Soviet System," *Political Quarterly* 58 (April-June 1987): 139-151; and Ellen Jones and Benjamin Woodbury, "Chernobyl and Glasnost," *Problems of Communism* 35 (November-December 1986): 28-39.

10. Cited by I. F. Stone in *Nation*, February 28, 1987, p. 241.

11. Quoted in Brown, "Gorbachev and Reform," p. 148.

12. *New York Times*, April 23, 1987.

13. *Pravda*, February 6, 1987.

14. *Washington Post*, April 26, 1987.

15. Interviewed in *Izvestia*, November 3, 1988, p. 3; translated in *CDSP*, November 30, 1988, pp. 1-3.

16. S. Frederick Starr, "Soviet Union: A Civil Society," *Foreign Policy*, no. 70 (Spring 1988): 26-41.

17. *New York Times*, April 30, 1988.

18. *Washington Post*, July 1, 1987, p. A1.

19. Brown, "Gorbachev and Reform," p. 148.

20. Vladimir Kusin, "What Gorbachev's Reforms Mean for Eastern Europe," Radio Free Europe Research *Background Report* (hereafter RFER) 10, February 5, 1987.

21. Marshall Goldman, "Gorbachev's Plan," *New York Times*, August 2, 1987, p. F3.

22. TASS, June 26, 1987.

23. Jacek Kuron, "Gorbachev: The View from Warsaw," *Harpers*, July 1987, p. 27.

24. *Kommunist*, October 1988, pp. 22-33; translated in *CDSP*, December 7, 1988, pp. 1-5.

25. *Pravda*, November 18, 1988, p. 3; translated in *CDSP*, December 21, 1988, p. 1.

26. Yevgeniy Primakov, "A New Philosophy of Foreign Policy," *Pravda*, July 10, 1987, p. 4; translated in *CDSP*, August 12, 1987, pp. 1-4.

27. *Pravda*, July 26, 1988, p. 4; translated in *CDSP*, August 24, 1988, pp. 13-14.

28. *Izvestia*, November 18, 1988, p. 5; translated in *CDSP*, December 14, 1988, p. 1.

29. *New York Times*, January 19, 1989, p. A4.

30. V. I. Dashichev in *Komsomolskaya Pravda*, June 19, 1988, p. 3; translated in *CDSP*, July 27, 1988, p. 29.

31. This section is drawn in part from David S. Mason, "Glasnost, Perestroika and Eastern Europe," *International Affairs* 64 (Summer 1988): 431-448.

32. Gorlin, "The Soviet Economy," p. 326.
33. Kusin, "What Gorbachev's Reforms Mean," p. 42.
34. Professor Leonid Abalkin, Director of the Institute of Economics of the Soviet Academy of Sciences; cited in RFER, *Yugoslav Situation Report* 3, May 4, 1987.
35. For a comparison of East European growth rates, see Zbigniew Fallenbuchl, "The CMEA and Eastern Europe," *International Journal* 43 (Winter 1987): 115.
36. See Seweryn Bialer and Joan Afferica, "The Genesis of Gorbachev's World," *Foreign Affairs: America and the World 1985* 64, no. 3 (1986): 612.
37. *Pravda*, May 27, 1987.
38. For example, during Yegor Ligachev's recent press conference in Hungary; *Pravda*, April 26, 1987.
39. As reported in the Polish daily *Zycie Warszawy*, February 7-8, 1987, p. 5.
40. *Pravda*, April 11, 1987, pp. 1-2; emphasis added.
41. *Pravda*, May 27, 1987.
42. See RFER, *Background Report* 43, March 25, 1987.
43. Charles Gati, "Gorbachev and Eastern Europe," *Foreign Affairs*, Summer 1987: 958-975.
44. Politburo member Imre Pozsgay in a Hungarian radio interview; reported in the *San Francisco Examiner*, January 29, 1989.
45. *Pravda*, April 22, 1987, p. 1.
46. Mieczyslaw Rakowski cited in RFER, Polish Situation Report/3, March 12, 1987.
47. *Polityka*, July 11, 1987, p. 11.
48. *Wall Street Journal*, July 30, 1987, p. 14.
49. *Kommunist*, September 1986; cited in Karen Dawisha and Jonathan Valdez, "Socialist Internationalism in Eastern Europe," *Problems of Communism* 36 (March-April 1987): 12-13.
50. *Wall Street Journal*, July 30, 1987, p. 14.
51. Quoted in the *Washington Post*, April 7, 1987.
52. *Wall Street Journal*, July 23, 1987.
53. *Polityka*, January 16, 1988; cited in RFER PSR/5, April 11, 1988, p. 13.
54. RFER, PSR/5, April 11, 1988, p. 13.
55. RFER, *Polish Situation Report* 4, April 10, 1987.
56. RFER, PSR/3, February 25, 1988, p. 19.
57. *Pravda*, May 22, 1987, p. 4.
58. Cited in the *Christian Science Monitor*, July 11, 1988.
59. Cited in the *New York Times*, May 29, 1988, p. A18.
60. RFER, *Background Report* 139, July 21, 1988.
61. RFER, PSR, February 25, 1988 and April 11, 1988.
62. See David Mason and Dan Nelson, "Political Apathy in Poland," *Studium Papers* 12 (July 1988): 68-71.

63. In the underground publication *KOS*, April 22, 1988; translated in *East European Reporter* 3 (Autumn 1988): 36.
64. Survey cited in RFER, *Background Report* 119, June 28, 1988, p. 20.
65. *International Herald Tribune*, October 14, 1988.
66. RFER, PSR/19, December 16, 1988, p. 16.
67. Text of the resolution in the *New York Times*, January 20, 1989, p. A5.
68. *Pravda*, July 12, 1988, p. 1; translated in *CDSP*, August 10, 1988, p. 13.
69. *Pravda*, July 15, 1988, pp. 1-2; translated in *CDSP*, August 10, 1988, p. 15.
70. *Christian Science Monitor*, July 14, 1988.
71. *Christian Science Monitor*, July 11, 1988.
72. *Izvestia*, September 17, 1988; translated in *CDSP*, October 5, 1988, pp. 11-12.
73. *Pravda*, September 2, 1988, p. 7; translated in *CDSP*, September 28, 1988, p. 22.
74. Reported in the *New York Times*, September 17, 1988, p. 4.
75. "Sovereignty and the Internationalist Obligations of Socialist Countries," *Pravda*, September 26, 1968, p. 4; translated in *CDSP*, October 16, 1968, pp. 10-12.
76. The following few paragraphs are adapted from Mason, "Glasnost, Perestroika and Eastern Europe."
77. RFER, *Background Report* 1, January 3, 1987.
78. RFER, Czechoslovak Situation Report/2, February 6, 1987.
79. *Pravda*, April 11, 1987, pp. 1-2.
80. See Vladimir Kusin, "Gustav Husak's Strange Absence from the Moscow Parade," RFER *Background Report* 219, November 12, 1987.
81. RFER *Background Report* 244, December 23, 1987.
82. Quoted in RFER, CSR/1, January 21, 1988.
83. Quoted in RFER, CSR/2, February 15, 1988.
84. Cited in RFER *Background Report* 121, June 29, 1988.
85. RFER CSR/5, March 25, 1988.
86. For description of the reforms, see Dawisha and Valdez, "Socialist Internationalism," pp. 4 and 10; and RFER, CSR/1, January 17, 1987.
87. Prime Minister Strougal, quoted in the *New York Times*, July 8, 1988, p. A4.
88. RFER CSR/5, March, 25, 1988.
89. Interview with Jakes in *Time*, April 18, 1988.
90. *Rude Pravo*, June 29, 1987; translated in *Daily Report-East Europe* (Foreign Broadcast Information Service, hereafter FBIS), July 8, 1987.
91. *Christian Science Monitor*, October 2, 1987, p. 7.
92. *Christian Science Monitor*, August 17, 1988, pp. 1, 9.
93. *New York Times*, October 28, 1988, p. A13.

94. RFER, CSR/9, June 28, 1988, p. 21.

95. Quoted in *Christian Science Monitor*, August 17, 1988, p. 9.

96. Interview on Austrian television, July 8, 1988; quoted in RFER CSR/10, July 14, 1988, p. 3.

97. Josef Brada highlights the many similarities between the new Czechoslovak economic reforms and those of 1968 in his "Soviet Reforms and East European Responses," a paper presented at a conference on New Dimensions of the Polish Economy, Wichita, Kansas, October 1987.

98. *New York Times*, April 4, 1987.

99. *Rude Pravo*, June 19, 1987; translated in *Daily Report-Eastern Europe* (FBIS), July 2, 1987.

100. Speech by party leader Jakes reprinted in *Pravda*, February 25, 1988.

101. *New York Times*, November 4, 1987, pp. 75-76; cited in Aurel Braun, "Whither the Warsaw Pact in the Gorbachev Era?" *International Journal* 43 (Winter 1987-88): 63-105.

102. Gennadi Gerasimov, quoted in Gati, "Gorbachev and Eastern Europe," p. 972.

103. Cited in RFER, CSR/3, March 1, 1988.

104. *Moskovskiye Novosti*, August 28, 1988, pp. 6-7; translated in *CDSP*, September 21, 1988, p. 7.

105. Ibid.

106. Quoted in Mark Uhlig, "Prague Waits for a Thaw," *New York Times Magazine*, September 4, 1988, p. 28.

107. A phrase employed by the Krakow sociologist Jacek Wasilewski, in a presentation at Stanford University, February 2, 1989.

108. Milan Kundera, "The Tragedy of Central Europe," *New York Review of Books*, April 26, 1984, pp. 33-38.

109. See Alex Pravda, "In the Eastern Bloc," *Los Angeles Times*, August 23, 1988.

110. Janos Hoos, chief of Hungarian National Planning Board, quoted in the *Washington Post*, April 6, 1987.

111. On this issue, see Tony Judt, "The Dilemmas of Dissidence: The Politics of Opposition in East-Central Europe," *Eastern European Politics and Societies* 2 (Spring 1988): 200-201; J. F. Brown, "A Western Overview" [of the Soviet-U.S. Conference on Eastern Europe], *Problems of Communism* 37 (May-August 1988): 57; and data from the Soviet émigré project in Brian Silver, "Political Beliefs of the Soviet Citizen," in *Politics, Work, and Daily Life in the USSR*, ed. James Millar (Cambridge: Cambridge University Press, 1987), especially pp. 108-114.

112. Judt, "The Dilemmas," p. 239.

CHAPTER 2

Developing Socialism in the Soviet Union and China

J. RICHARD WALSH

While Soviet views of Chinese reforms moved from hostility to greater receptivity, Mikhail Gorbachev has made improved relations with China a keystone of his "new thinking" in foreign policy. Since the initiation of glasnost and perestroika under Gorbachev, the Chinese have increasingly drawn comparisons between the Soviet Union and the People's Republic of China (PRC). In Gorbachev's reforms the Chinese see less theoretical determinism and greater pragmatism, a willingness to follow Deng Xiaoping's oft-quoted admonition "to seek the truth from the facts."

Paralleling their leadership's own ideological justifications for reforms, Chinese analysts note the Soviet regime's claim to be in a period of developing socialism, though without being a "developing socialist state" like China.[1] As a Soviet party official observed, the difference is that China is a developing country making the transition from capitalism to socialism and this allows it to be more inventive. He concluded that "it's much more difficult for us to abandon our socialist ideology."[2] The shorter historical roots of socialism in China and the deeper roots of entrepreneurship among the Chinese people made it easier for Deng to initiate economic reforms. After embracing economic reforms sooner and more readily than the Soviet Union, China has been more cautious about initiating the political and cultural reforms that the Soviet leadership deems primary for unleashing the initiative and creativity of the people. Although the starting point for reforms in each country is different, the strong commitment of Deng and Gorbachev to greater openness and the restructuring of their economies creates the possibility of convergent reform strategies.

An analysis of this convergence rests on a consideration of a complex mix of political-ideological, economic, and strategic factors.[3] From the late 1950s until the late 1970s ideological differences shaped Chinese condemnations of Soviet "revisionism" and "hegemonism." In the post-Mao period, the Chinese leadership has continually relied upon Soviet socialism as a means to legitimize their own socialist regime. As Gilbert Rozman notes, the history of Chinese socialism provides little support for Deng Xiaoping's reform program. Soviet history is replete with supportive examples from Lenin's New Economic Policy, to Stalin's education policies and emphasis on technology, to Brezhnev's support of a "socialist way of life."[4] Beginning in 1979 much effort went into transforming Chinese understanding of 60 years of Soviet history to the advantage of an emerging view of "socialism with Chinese characteristics."

For both Soviet and Chinese policy makers the growth of economic relations is a logical outcome of their common roots in a model of economic development and a means to promote a desirable level of cooperation. As several economic agreements attest, there is a basis for this cooperation. However, years of conflict and reform have altered the compatibility of their economies. By the early 1980s, over 80 percent of China's trade was with Western nations and East Asian newly industrializing countries. Nonetheless, the Soviet Union represents a market for Chinese primary goods, while China is a market for selected Soviet technologies. Bilateral economic relations can be conducted on the basis of barter trade, avoiding a drain on hard currency reserves. Finally, there is a growing mutual interest in each other's economic experiences that could lay the basis for broader economic relations in the future.[5]

The third set of factors relates to strategic and geopolitical issues that have impacted on bilateral relations. Since the late 1950s, both the Soviet Union and China have allowed conflictual foreign relations to determine evaluations of each other. Only in the early 1980s did conflict begin to abate in part due to Chinese disillusionment with the Reagan administration and desires for a more independent foreign policy, Deng's consolidation of power, and the prospect of leadership change in the Soviet Union. A Soviet impetus to more normalized relations came from Leonid Brezhnev's March 1982 speech in Tashkent where he called for greater Sino-Soviet cooperation. Continual high-level bilateral talks on normalized relations ensued while scientific and cultural exchanges and border trade steadily increased.

Growing Sino-Soviet interdependence reflects the mutual need for a peaceful international environment in order to concentrate resources on domestic economic reform. However, China is concerned about its ability to control the pace of normalization and has maintained "the three obstacles" (border issues, the Soviet invasion of Afghanistan, and Vietnamese occupation of Cambodia) as leverage. This has not deterred Gorbachev from his continual wooing of China and gradual removal of the obstacles through changes in Soviet policy.

In this chapter, I will examine Chinese perceptions of socialist development in the USSR and the growing reciprocity in economic and strategic relations using the three sets of factors outlined above. In the Gorbachev era, political-ideological and economic factors are becoming more important determinants of bilateral relations. Chinese analysis of Soviet ideological adaptation and domestic economic problems has become more systematic as the Soviets have demonstrated the willingness to accommodate "socialism with Chinese characteristics." Understanding of the Soviet Union's chronic and fundamental economic problems coupled with a changing international environment has resulted in a greater Chinese appreciation of the Soviet need for a more stable external environment. Though geopolitical tensions persist, the Chinese view is increasingly one of a Soviet Union of reduced global capabilities and hegemonic intentions.

VIEWING SOVIET IDEOLOGICAL CHANGE AND POLITICAL REFORMS

As the post-Mao leadership began the process of the de-Maoification of China, ideological conflict with the Soviet Union became less acute as ideology became a basis for potential cooperation. The growing importance of ideological factors is evident in two ways. First is the growing sense of shared experience with positive Chinese assessments of Soviet reforms and yet questions about their possible relevance for China. Second, there is the possibility of restoring party-to-party ties, a process initiated by the Soviets when Brezhnev recognized China as a socialist country in 1982. Both aspects of ideological/political relations are discussed below.

In the period prior to Gorbachev's rise to power, assessments about the Soviet experience were mixed; that is, negative enough to support China's foreign policy while positive enough to attest to the superiority of socialism. By the early 1980s, China's Soviet watchers came to some conclusions as to the direction of Soviet ideological development. These observers believed that the Soviets had come to accept the equality among communist states and shared with the Chinese the challenge of acquiring from the West needed aid and technology while protecting their own ideology and institutions.[6]

Paralleling the importance that the Chinese attach to Deng Xiaoping's leadership, China began to measure the possibility of convergent reform strategies with the rise of Mikhail Gorbachev. His openness in addressing the magnitude of problems facing the USSR caught the attention of Chinese observers who noted differences between Gorbachev and his predecessors. Early Chinese commentary on the prospects for reform in the Soviet Union stressed the lively debate on economic problems carried on by Soviet scholars in the press and academic journals. *People's Daily*, the newspaper of the Communist Party of China (CPC), quoted approvingly from *Pravda*, a publication of the Communist Party of the Soviet Union, when *Pravda* pointed out that "we [the Soviets] should test theoretical conclusions and the correctness of our policy decisions in a systematic manner through practice."[7]

Chinese analysts recognized the importance of the 27th Congress of the CPSU in February 1986 for establishing Gorbachev's reform program. The Chinese press monitored the development of the revised CPSU program that was presented to the 27th Congress. Gorbachev had set the tone for change at the CPSU Central Committee meeting in April 1985. By the fall of 1985, Chinese analysts were reporting that drafts of the CPSU program noted that reforms were to be achieved through the "all-around perfection of socialism." The wording became for the Chinese a fundamental indicator of Soviet intent since it represented an abandonment of the previous claim that the Soviet Union was in "the period of developed socialism." The emphasis on perfecting socialism meant the attempt to correct some of the unrealistic policies of the Khrushchev and Brezhnev eras.[8]

From the perspective of Chinese analysts the reform program presented at the 27th CPSU Congress marked the Soviet Union's entry into a new era of development. Analyses of Gorbachev's closing address to the Congress cited the ideological obstacles that stood in the way of accelerated development in the USSR. As noted by Gorbachev himself, the major reason for the lagging development was the failure to understand the urgency of reform. Soviet cadres suffered from the "bondages of outdated concepts" by allowing Marxism-Leninism to evolve into "stiff and ossified formulas and cure-all remedies for emergencies."[9]

In drawing the distinction between Gorbachev and his predecessors, Chinese observers elaborated on the ideological aspects of his reform program, noting the parallels with Chinese experience. By contrast with earlier reforms, Gorbachev's plan began with criticism of the "automatic-adaptation" theory, which states that once socialism is established the relations of production would automatically adapt to the productive forces and guarantee their rapid development. The present plan argues that socialist relations of production can lose their stimulating effect and become barriers to progress. The implication of this theoretical change means the deemphasis of collective relations and the encouragement of more autonomous cooperative and individual activities in the context of enhanced market forces.[10]

These new forms of relations parallel the Chinese introduction of the responsibility system and enterprise autonomy in the rural and urban sectors and as such represent fundamental reforms. But among Chinese analysts, there was a growing emphasis on the more formidable ideological obstacles the USSR faced in comparison to the PRC. Emphasis was in part due to the problems of ossified thinking that Gorbachev and other Soviet leaders continually cited. The January 1987 Plenum of the CPSU Central Committee was perceived as a major turning point in the fight against ossified thinking. From the Soviet point of view, the solution was more glasnost to strengthen the development of socialist democracy in order to tap the potential of the socialist system. Chinese commentators noted that the principle of glasnost was reaffirmed to direct popular attention against bureaucratic obstacles to reform.[11] This reaffirmation paralleled Chinese concerns about "bureaucratism" in their own society. However, the emphasis on openness and democratization highlighted the different starting points of Soviet and Chinese reforms.

As the Soviets continued to push glasnost and political reform through 1987 and into 1988, one could observe a divergence of opinion occurring between official and unofficial commentary. Official government commentary on the course of Soviet reforms tended to be more cautious in its assessments, suggesting that the irreversibility of Soviet reforms was an open question. It seemed that the more Gorbachev pressed for political reform the more often official Chinese commentary noted the resistance to changes and the gap between the formulation and implementation of policy.

This more skeptical tone was clearly evident in official commentary on the CPSU party conference in June 1988 that adopted several resolutions relating to political reform. Commentary issued by the New China News Agency (NCNA) declared that the CPSU "has to decide whether to push reform forward or let it fall through, as in the 1950s and the 1960s." NCNA did not compare the accomplishments of Chinese economic reforms and nascent efforts to divorce the CPC from state administration with Gorbachev's initiatives. Rather, commentary focused on the obstacles facing the Soviets and how far reforms must go before affecting the plight of the average Soviet citizen. The NCNA report noted that the major task for the near future is "quick, comprehensive reform of the entire economic mechanism." According to the press agency's Moscow correspondent, it was the hope of the Soviet people that the conference would adopt measures that would make reform irreversible.[12]

Among other Chinese observers there has been a more sanguine view of Soviet reforms and their prospects. As Su Shaozhi, one of China's leading Marxist theorists, noted, Soviet reform was becoming a new focus of attention for the development and creative application of Marxism. At a seminar conducted by China's Soviet Economic Research Association in the fall of 1986, participants agreed that Soviet economic theory had tended to lag behind actual practice and thus was one of the greatest obstacles to reform. However, by rejecting the "automatic adaptation" theory noted above and by conceding that market regulation still functions in a socialist society, Soviet theorists were making progress toward synchronized economic and political reforms.[13]

Political reforms in the Soviet Union were increasingly capturing the attention of Chinese intellectuals. The CPSU's emphasis on political reforms at its January 1987 plenary session coincided with the aborted attempt of Chinese intellectuals and students and some CPC leaders, most notably General Secretary Hu Yaobang, to place democratic reforms more prominently on the political agenda. Despite attempts to limit the role of the CPC and strengthen the independent role of the National People's Congress, for many Chinese intellectuals there was no genuine forum for public debate and criticism like that developing in the USSR. CPC members did not disagree with each other in public, while news reports were carefully screened before publication under the formula of 80 percent good news and 20 percent bad. University students were largely prevented from demonstrating for better living conditions or for democracy.

Reflecting the views of outspoken Chinese reformers who desired more pluralism to ensure the progress of reforms, Xia Yan, vice-chairman of the China Federation of Literary and Art Circles, stated in an interview with the Shanghai's *World Economic Herald* that "the Soviet Union has marched faster than us in the ideological field. Gorbachev's openness is more thorough than our transparency."[14] In the same Shanghai publication, a June 1988 interview with the editor in chief of *Pravda* underlined the point of Soviet ideological progress and invited the Chinese to learn from the Soviets. Recognizing Chinese economic successes, *Pravda* editor Viktor G. Afanasyev posited the idea of a mutual learning process. His impression was that the restrictions on the Chinese press formed a sharp contrast to the greater openness and freedom of the Chinese economy. Therefore, he suggested that "the Soviet Union should learn from China's economic circles, while China should learn from Soviet press circles."[15]

The events surrounding the student-led democracy movement of April–June 1989 indicate that the desires for political reforms, partly inspired by the Soviet experience, were widespread among Chinese intellectuals.[16] At the close of the 1989 session of the National People's Congress and on the eve of the democracy movement, Premier Li Peng stated that the Chinese government would not consider appeals from intellectuals for political reforms that might jeopardize social stability. Premier Li said that democratization in China would proceed slowly and China would not follow the example of the Soviet Union, which held its first competitive elections in March 1989. He argued that the situation was different in China and that his nation, "cannot mechanically copy measures or policies adopted by the Soviet Union."[17]

By the spring of 1989, however, much as the Chinese government might disagree with the adoption of more Soviet-style openness, the second aspect of ideological/political relations with the Soviet Union was gaining momentum, namely party-to-party relations. Under Gorbachev, Soviet attitudes toward the international communist movement appear to be changing. In his report to the 27th CPSU

Congress in February 1986, Gorbachev affirmed that the unity of an international movement "has nothing in common with uniformity, hierarchy," that it does not mean "one party's claim to monopolize the truth." Soviet spokespersons frequently associated improving Sino-Soviet relations with unity within the international socialist movement. China's continuing commitment to a Marxist worldview and attachment to the notion of an international movement left open the prospect of greater ideological rapprochement through normalized party-to-party relations.[18]

With the Soviet Union's blessing, East European communist parties established ties with the CPC beginning in 1986 (Poland and East Germany) and concluding with Premier Zhao Ziyang's tour of Eastern Europe in 1987 (Hungary, Czechoslovakia, and Bulgaria). The Soviet leadership permitted its allies to establish party ties with China as a means to pave relations between the CPSU and the CPC. Soviet interest in party-to-party relations was also indicated by an unprecedented *Pravda* article published on July 1, 1986, the 65th anniversary of the founding of the CPC. The article gave a very complementary account of CPC history and drew from Lenin's work on imperialism to explain the difficult situation in which the CPC was founded and the subsequent "zig-zags" in its historical development.[19]

In October and November 1987, as further indication of growing party-to-party ties, correspondents from *Pravda* and *Kommunist*, the theoretical journal of the CPSU Central Committee, covered the 13th Congress of the CPC in October, and the CPC acknowledged a congratulatory message from the CPSU Central Committee. China reciprocated by sending representatives from the China-USSR Friendship Association to Moscow for the 70th anniversary of the October Revolution, the first such representation in years.[20]

There appears to be an ideological imperative at work that could culminate in the normalization of party ties. If one-party rule is predicated on the global historical validity of Marxism-Leninism, what Deng Xiaoping refers to as one of the "four cardinal principles," then ties with similar regimes are important. A Sino-Soviet reconciliation could strengthen Gorbachev's position at home by making it more difficult to characterize him as ideologically unorthodox. Finally, given the mutual concern for preserving an international communist movement of some sort, the recent decline of nonruling communist parties in the West and the challenges facing socialist regimes in the East make the reestablishment of Sino-Soviet party ties more compelling.[21]

Efforts to establish ties between the CPC and CPSU have culminated in an agreement during the May 1989 Sino-Soviet summit to develop contacts and exchanges. Development will be in accordance "with the principles of independence, complete equality, mutual respect, and noninterference in each other's affairs."[22] These are the same principles that are the basis of normalized ties between the CPC and East European parties and those of which Gorbachev has repeatedly spoken and applied since February 1986. What can give further impetus to these contacts are the growing parallels in economic reforms and bilateral economic ties.

ECONOMIC RELATIONS AND ECONOMIC MODELS

Since the early 1980s, the trend in both Chinese and Soviet economic policy and development has been toward expanded economic relations. Aspects of these relations include a tenfold increase in trade in the past decade, growing scientific and technological cooperation, mutual investment opportunities, and Soviet interest in China's economic strategy. Although many of these developments predate Gorbachev's rise to power, a growing belief in the efficacy of Chinese reforms and the mutual benefits that accrue from economic ties gave greater impetus to economic relations since the mid-1980s.

Economic ties between the PRC and USSR are evolving along three lines: a long-term trade agreement, scientific and technological cooperation, and the expansion of border trade. One of the foundations for economic cooperation is the long-term trade agreement signed in 1985 that established trade on the basis of equality and mutual benefit. Barter trade is the mainstay of bilateral relations with the Swiss franc as the unit of accounting. From 1985 to early 1989, bilateral trade was valued at 12 billion francs. Raw materials and primary products account for 70 percent of trade and finished products 30 percent. The Soviet Union exports electric power, mining and chemical equipment, motor vehicles, aircraft, electric locomotives and railway carriages, ferrous and nonferrous metals, timber, and other industrial materials. In return the Soviets import from China tungsten ore, foodstuffs, cotton cloth, knitted goods, and other industrial goods and materials.[23]

Beginning in 1983, China and the Soviet Union began identifying projects for cooperation in the spheres of metallurgy; coal, oil, and gas production; chemical, textile, and production industries; and railway transport. Cooperation was formalized with the signing of a 1985 agreement that covered the construction and transformation of industrial projects and established the Joint Committee for Economic, Trade, Scientific, and Technological Cooperation. As of early 1989, 50 contracts for transforming and developing new projects had been signed.[24]

During the 1950s, the Soviet Union aided China in the construction of 156 large-scale industrial projects. After some 30 years of use, these projects are in severe need of technological updating. The Soviet government has dispatched a group of experts to help the Chinese assess how best to transform them. To date the largest transformation projects will be undertaken at steelworks in Wushan and Anshan, the Luoyang bearing plant, a paper pulp mill and a flax factory in Harbin. Future cooperation will be concentrated in the areas of electronics, ferrous and nonferrous metals, chemicals, textiles, and transport. New projects that concentrate on infrastructure problems include thermal power plants and transmission lines and railway projects in northeast and southern China.[25]

Border trade between the two countries serves as an important supplement for trade conducted through government agreements. Trade between the Soviet Union and the Chinese provinces of Xinjiang, Inner Mongolia, and Heilongjiang has developed very quickly since 1983. According to Soviet figures, in 1988 border trade increased some 200 percent over 1987 with trade valued at 600 million Swiss francs moving through Heilongjiang and Xinjiang provinces alone.[26] Both of these provinces are allowed to conduct trade talks with the Soviet Union. This concession is intended to compensate for the more profitable freedom granted to China's coastal provinces to make trade and investment deals with Western and other Asian nations. In July 1988 the PRC announced the right of local governments to conduct barter trade with the Soviet Union, thereby expanding the number of open trading cities in the border areas. As well, participation was broadened to include China's inner and maritime provinces. Delegations from the south of China are turning up in the border city of Heihe to negotiate barter deals and joint ventures with the Soviets. In 1988 some 75 percent of the goods exported from Heilongjiang province were produced by joint ventures, cooperative enterprises, or companies processing imported materials. In order to capitalize on the trend toward joint ventures and the establishment of a direct rail line, Blagoveshchensk, an industrial town on the Amur River, has asked Moscow for permission to establish a Chinese-style special economic zone.[27]

The significant increase in Sino-Soviet trade and the particular contacts generated by the border trade may represent the beginning of Gorbachev's own open-door policy for foreign trade and investment in the Soviet Far East. However, the difficulty of calculating barter equivalents places restraints on trade despite the benefits. Additionally, there are concerns on both sides of the border about the expansion of trade without significant economic reforms in the Soviet Union. Soviet goods are of poor quality and deliveries are often late. In order to rectify these problems, the Soviets have been paying closer attention to Chinese economic reforms.

Soviet discussions about Chinese reforms have been shaped by three concerns that parallel Chinese concerns about Soviet reforms.[28] The first is to justify current Soviet policy toward China. Soviet policy had made the transition from the negative polemics of the 1960s and 1970s to the policy under Gorbachev of improving ties with the PRC. Consequently, Soviet commentary expresses understanding and respect for Chinese efforts to develop a socialist society.

The second function of Soviet analysis is to explain current Chinese policy and anticipate future developments. The opinions of Soviet commentators and analysts have been divided. Articles in the major publications have generally been at the least neutral, and at the most positively disposed toward Chinese reforms. This is in keeping with the general foreign policy line of the Soviet leadership. However, analysts associated with the Far East Institute tended to be more negative in highlighting the difficulty the PRC was having in developing a strategy that was both socialist and capable of overcoming China's underdevelopment. By the summer of 1987, the tone of these analysts' arguments was changing. The head of the China department of the Institute was quoted as saying that reform in China was "vitally important" to the Soviet Union and that the Soviets "now look at [China's] reforms as if it were our own business."[29] The publication of a selection of Deng Xiaoping's works in Russian in January 1988 indicated the triumph of the more positive view of

Chinese reforms. As one reviewer wrote in *Moscow News*, there is "a special significance for understanding the perestroika attached to the Chinese experience."[30]

Third, one can see in Soviet discussions of Chinese reform commentary on possible reforms of the Soviet system. Chinese analysis of Soviet and East European reform has played the same function by giving insights into debates of internal policy. So too in the Soviet Union where Feodor Burlatskiy, a frequent commentator on Chinese affairs, made the explicit connection in 1986 when he noted: "I am deeply convinced that Gorbachev has already launched the country on a path of reform comparable to that of the Chinese."[31] Two areas of Chinese reform have received the continual attention of Soviet analysts, special economic zones and decollectivization of agriculture.

In order to attract foreign investment, China established special economic zones (SEZs) in two coastal provinces in 1979. Foreign investors operating in these zones enjoy preferential tax treatment and other advantages in order to attract joint-equity ventures. China's SEZs provide Soviet analysts an opportunity to investigate means to achieve Gorbachev's stated goal of creating an export-oriented economy in the Soviet Far East. Soviet analysts have differed in their assessments of the SEZs, suggesting that Gorbachev's attempts to open the Soviet economy are controversial.[32] However, by the summer of 1988, Ivan Ivanov, the deputy chairman of the Soviet State Committee for Foreign Economic Relations, was telling a delegation of Macao businessmen that "your knowledge and experience in China's special economic zones are helpful to the Soviet Union in drafting the Law on Special Economic Zones. . . ." He continued by saying that the Soviet Union would adopt relevant Chinese economic forms, in particular the joint venture.[33]

The collective farm system, which is the backbone of Soviet agriculture, has been virtually dismantled in China and replaced by a responsibility system of contracts and land leasing. The response has been a huge increase in productivity and the development of rural industry to absorb excess labor. Unlike the Soviet Union, China has succeeded in feeding its population. Therefore, according to Leonid Abalkin, director of the Soviet Institute of Economics, "the fast and successful development of agriculture through broad application of the family-responsibility system presents special interest to us."[34]

Both Chinese and Soviet analysts note the differences between the Soviet and Chinese experience—that is, the imperative for reform in

China after the Cultural Revolution and the deep roots of Soviet collective agriculture with its economies of scale and higher level of mechanization. Nonetheless, Soviet analysts and officials contend that the Chinese experience could be broadly applied to the Soviet Union. As First Vice-Chairman Peotr Pesker of the Soviet State Planning Commission stated in an interview with the Chinese news agency *Xinhua*, "The food shortage could basically be solved if the soviets follow China's contract and leasing system."[35] In March 1989 the CPSU Central Committee agreed to allow farmers to take out leases on land like their Chinese counterparts.

To the need to attract foreign capital and decollectivize agriculture one can add two additional parallels between the Soviet and Chinese reform strategies: a "dual track" combining some measure of market forces with centralized planning and the reduced priority of the defense sector.[36] These four parallels and the growing economic ties between the two countries provide the basis for continued mutual understanding and cooperation. Both countries share the need to concentrate resources on domestic reforms and consequently need a peaceful international environment. Strategic concerns and conflicts appear to be abating due to China's independent foreign policy and the Soviet Union's "new thinking."

FROM HEGEMONISM TO "NEW THINKING"

Since its origins in the Shanghai Communiqué in 1972, China has continually used the term "hegemonism" to describe the international behavior of the Soviet Union. The term describes a superpower with the intention and capability to project its power globally and use force if necessary to meet its objectives. Through the early 1980s, Chinese commentators and analysts overwhelmingly placed emphasis on the dangers of Soviet hegemonism. However, beginning in 1981, one can find some differing opinions among Chinese analysts who noted Soviet domestic economic weaknesses and the possible constraints on Soviet objectives. At least one Chinese analyst in early 1983 went so far as to suggest that the Soviet leadership might desire a more peaceful international environment, which would include the reduction of Sino-Soviet tensions.[37]

Gorbachev inherited both the domestic economic problems with their potential constraints and a foreign policy of improving relations with China. Since the resumption of normalization talks with China in 1982, the Soviets have generally portrayed the development of relations optimistically. Events in 1985—the long-term trade and scientific-technological agreements—appeared to support the Soviets' optimistic assessment and anticipation that progress could continue without major Soviet concessions. By early 1986, though, the issue of concessions came to a head. Since 1982 the Chinese have maintained their three obstacles to normalization: reduction of Soviet troops along their mutual border and their removal from Mongolia, withdrawal of Soviet troops from Afghanistan, and Soviet pressure on Vietnam to give up control of Cambodia. In contrast with his Soviet counterpart's more optimistic views, in January 1986 then Deputy Foreign Minister Qian Qichen chided the USSR for attempting "under various pretexts to dodge discussions on ways to remove these obstacles," and described China's commitment to them as "unshakable."[38]

In the face of Chinese skepticism Gorbachev took the offensive. In his report to the 27th Congress of the CPSU in February 1986 he emphasized the extent of improvement and potential for Sino-Soviet cooperation. At the eighth round of normalization talks held in Moscow in April 1986, Soviet Foreign Minister Eduard Shevardnadze suggested to the Chinese envoy the possibility of a summit between the countries' top leaders. The Chinese rejected the offer as "unrealistic" before the removal of the three obstacles. In a speech in Vladivostok on July 28, Gorbachev directly addressed two of the obstacles by announcing the gradual withdrawal of Soviet troops from Afghanistan, discussions with Mongolian leaders to remove most of the troops from that country, and the willingness to discuss other reductions on a "proportional and balanced basis." Finally, Gorbachev agreed to accept China's claim to draw the boundary down the main channels of the Amur and Ussuri rivers in order to resume negotiations on the boundary disputes.[39]

The Soviets had obviously abandoned the belief of progress toward normalization without concessions and had placed China in the position of having to react to Gorbachev's initative. China's Foreign Minister Wu Xueqian welcomed Gorbachev's ideas for improving relations but noted that he had sidestepped the issue of Vietnam's occupation of Cambodia. Recognizing the need to regain control over the pace of normalization, in a September 1986 interview with an American reporter, Deng Xiaoping said that China had "expressed cautious welcome to what was new and positive" in Gorbachev's Vladivostok speech. But in a notable change of emphasis, Deng stated that the end to Vietnamese occupation was the "main obstacle in Sino-Soviet relations." If Gorbachev could remove this obstacle, then Deng would go anywhere in the Soviet Union to meet with Gorbachev.[40] Subsequent to his remarks, the Chinese raised contact with the Soviets to the vice-ministerial level and agreed to resume boundary talks in February 1987.

Was there now substance to Gorbachev's "new thinking"? Building on the thesis of economic constraints on Soviet behavior posited in the early 1980s, Chinese analysts began to take a closer look at the new Soviet pragmatism. In a piece published in *World Affairs*, one Chinese analyst argued that the changes in Soviet thinking were as much due to the need to adapt to the changing international situation as to Soviet domestic problems. His summary of the substance of the "new thinking" emphasized the growing multipolarity and global interdependence that forced the Soviets to change their definition of security to one of greater global concern, to view East-West relations in less conflictual terms, to pursue a less ideological foreign policy, and to be more flexible in the conduct of policy.[41] An implication drawn from this analysis is that Chinese insistence on the removal of the three obstacles of global concern could influence Soviet behavior. Consequently, China's leaders continued to appear cautious and to insist that Sino-Soviet relations were far from being normalized despite the border talks and the development of economic, scientific, and cultural exchanges.

From 1987 to 1989 progress occurred on the issues outlined by Gorbachev in his July 1986 speech. In January 1987 the Soviets announced troop reductions in Mongolia that eventually led to a decision to the pullout of 75 percent of the troops stationed there. In April 1988 the USSR signed an accord in Geneva to withdraw Soviet forces from Afghanistan by February 1989. By the third round of the border talks in October 1987, both the PRC and the USSR had reached agreement on most of the eastern sections of the border and were beginning to turn their attention to the western regions. In December 1987 the Soviet Union signed the Intermediate Nuclear Forces treaty, which included the removal of all intermediate-range Soviet missiles from Asia in part to meet China's security concerns. In a January 1988 interview with the Chinese weekly *Outlook*, Gorbachev noted that the logical conclusion of these accomplishments and other ongoing political dialogues was a Sino-Soviet summit.[42]

Chinese spokespersons again rejected the call for a summit as premature, especially since the Cambodian issue remained unresolved. Since the Vladivostok speech, though, the Soviet position had changed substantially. In the summer of 1987 the Soviet Union adopted a more active role in promoting a Cambodian settlement. The Soviets agreed to the inclusion of the Chinese-backed Khmer Rouge faction in negotiations over a coalition government and apparently played a key role in persuading the Phnom Penh regime to negotiate with the exiled Prince Sihanouk. Gorbachev also encouraged Vietnam to support Sino-Soviet normalization and to improve its own relations with the PRC.[43] By the twelfth round of Sino-Soviet normalization talks in June 1988 the Cambodian issue had become the central issue and China agreed to the Soviet proposal to hold special negotiations on the issue.

The outcome of those negotiations on Cambodia in late August 1988 was a recognition that differences existed but both sides had "found common ground."[44] Common ground was not officially defined until February 1989; but it appeared that the last major barrier to full normalization was falling and momentum was building toward the first Sino-Soviet summit in 30 years. Despite the usual cautious statements to balance Soviet optimism, the Chinese were no longer rejecting the possibility of a summit meeting. Chinese spokespersons spent the fall of 1988 clarifying their position on a coalition government in Cambodia and securing a more moderate Khmer Rouge faction. Noting the progress in bilateral relations, Chinese analysts and commentators continually stated the advantages of full normalization for world peace and stability.[45]

From September 1988 until the issuing of a joint statement on the Cambodian issue in February 1989, the Chinese and Soviet foreign ministers conducted five rounds of talks on a Cambodian settlement. Although both sides announced that a summit meeting would take place during the first half of 1989, the dates of the summit, May 15–18, 1989, were not announced until February. It was reported in the Japanese press that the announcement of the date was held up by the Chinese until a joint statement was agreed upon. The statement, which was reconfirmed in the summit joint communiqué, noted the decision of the Vietnamese to withdraw from Cambodia by September 1989, the gradual reduction of military aid to all factions in Cambodia, the establishment of a provisional government under Prince Sihanouk, and the conduct of free elections under international supervision.[46]

Much can be attributed to Chinese insistence on the three obstacles as a factor that influenced changes in Soviet behavior and eventually led to a summit meeting in Beijing. However, one cannot overlook the substantive difference between Gorbachev and his predecessors that constitutes the "new thinking" in Soviet foreign policy. An integral part of this new approach is the willingness to seek a "balance of interests" that is more than just a tactically less rigid style. By setting a balance of interests as a goal, Gorbachev is raising the possibility that some traditional Soviet security interests can be sacrificed.[47] Gorbachev's willingness to address the three obstacles and present a vision of a new Asia-Pacific era is equally important for understanding the course of events from Vladivostok to Beijing.

CONCLUSION

Mikhail Gorbachev's pursuit of glasnost and perestroika does allow observers to draw similarities between the PRC and USSR. Paralleling their own claim to be "in the initial stage of socialism," the Chinese posit that both countries are in the global stage of developing socialism. Gorbachev's advocacy of international socialist pluralism should serve to strengthen potential ideological ties between the USSR and the PRC. As noted above, these ties have been important for legitimizing Chinese reforms.

The Soviet Union's eagerness to learn from the experience of Chinese economic reforms is clearly evident, but concerns do exist. One worry of reformers in the Soviet Union is that even with a more conducive climate for economic reform in China, reforms there have followed a cyclical pattern of advancement and retrenchment. By comparison, this suggests that with a population more resistant to change and a government less willing to decentralize decision making, Soviet economic reform may follow a more cyclical course.[48] If the past and present are indicators of the future, the methods of political adaptation that have been an integral part of glasnost—elections, a freer press, and political incorporation—will become increasingly important to the Soviet leadership. These methods provide the means to maintain the legitimacy of the regime while mediating the effects of economic reforms.[49]

Given the importance of glasnost to Soviet reform efforts and the repression of the democracy movement in China, it remains uncertain how much the Chinese are willing to learn from the Soviets. Gorbachev's emphasis on political reforms is seen officially as having little application to the Chinese polity. As one Chinese analyst from the Institute for Soviet and East European Studies argued, "China's cultural level is much lower than that of the Soviet Union. If the Chinese had the same freedoms as Soviets... the result would be anarchy."[50] The Chinese leadership continues to operate according to this assumption, ignoring Gorbachev's cautious praise of the students' democracy movement and repeated declarations during the May 1989 summit that economic change was impossible without political reform.[51] Despite these divergent attitudes, the Chinese leadership should not overlook the fact that Gorbachev has developed his reforms incrementally while not abandoning the central tenets of Marxism-Leninism.

So long as both countries remain preoccupied with domestic reforms, they will need stable relations with each other. There are limits to their rapprochement given Soviet military superiority and security ties with Vietnam and India, China's neighbors and rivals. However, the May 1989 summit should be viewed as an indication of China's confidence in its dealings with the Soviet Union, confidence nurtured by their mutual interests in economic reform and expanding economic relations. Gorbachev's visit to Beijing did not mark the beginning of normalization but how far the process has come.

Despite the progress that China and the Soviet Union have made, respectively, in economic and political reforms, the processes in both countries are at the early stages. The suppression of the democracy movement in June 1989 indicates possible setbacks in China's reforms, while in the Soviet Union the muddling-through in economic performance suggests that Gorbachev may be more popular abroad than at home. As such, both countries have only begun the task of developing socialism.

NOTES

1. For a discussion of the difference between developing socialism and a developing socialist state, see *Daily Report-China* (Foreign Broadcast Information Service, hereafter FBIS), September 9, 1987, p. 6.

2. Michael Dobbs, "A Historic, Tumultuous Summit," *Washington Post National Weekly Edition*, May 22-28, 1989, p. 7.

3. Herbert J. Ellison, "Changing Sino-Soviet Relations," *Problems of Communism* 36 (May-June 1987): 25.

4. Gilbert Rozman, *The Chinese Debate About Soviet Socialism, 1978-1985* (Princeton, NJ: Princeton University Press, 1987), p. 371.

5. Ellison, "Changing Relations," p. 28.

6. Rozman, *The Chinese View*, p. 22; and Rozman, "China's Soviet Watchers in the 1980s: A New Era of Scholarship," *World Politics* 37 (July 1985): 463-464.

7. *Daily Report-China* (FBIS), September 19, 1985, p. C2.

8. *Daily Report-China* (FBIS), September 30, 1985, p. C4; and December 9, 1985, p. C1.

9. *Daily Report-China* (FBIS), June 2, 1986, p. C3.

10. *Daily Report-China* (FBIS), January 9, 1987, p. C1; and Xi Lei, "Economic Reforms in the USSR—An Overview," *Beijing Review*, March 16, 1987, pp. 18-19.

11. *Daily Report-China* (FBIS), May 22, 1987, p. C4 and August 20, 1987, p. C3; Ding Yongning, "Chinese Journalists Look at Soviet Reforms," *Beijing Review*, September 21, 1987, p. 22.

12. Edward A. Gargan, "China Says Soviets Have a Way To Go," *New York Times*, June 30, 1988 p. 12; also see *Daily Report-China* (FBIS), July 18, 1988, p. 13.

13. *Daily Report-China* (FBIS), November 3, 1986, pp. C3-4.

14. *Daily Report-China* (FBIS), January 20, 1988, pp. 15-16.

15. *Daily Report-China* (FBIS), June 22, 1988, p. 8.

16. For a discussion of the roots of the most recent democracy movement in China among intellectuals, see Perry Link, "The Chinese Intellectuals and the Revolt," *New York Review of Books*, June 29, 1989, pp. 38-41.

17. Adi Ignatius, "Chinese Premier Rules Out Chance of Rapid Reforms," *Wall Street Journal*, April 4, 1989, p. A17.

18. Joan Barth Urban, "Gorbachev and the Communist World: Collapse or Perestroika?" *Problems of Communism* 37 (September-October 1988): 75.

19. Dan L. Strode, "Soviet China Policy in Flux," *Survival* 30 (July/August 1988): 339-340; for a translation of the *Pravda* article, see *Daily Report-Soviet Union* (FBIS) July 3, 1986, pp. B1-3.

20. Strode, "Soviet China Policy," p. 340.

21. Urban, "Perestroika or Collapse?" pp. 74 and 76.

22. "Sino-Soviet Joint Communiqué," *Beijing Review*, May 29-June 4, 1989, p. 16.

23. "Sino-Soviet Trade Booms," *Beijing Review*, January 30-February 5, 1989, p. 40; *Daily Report-China* (FBIS), July 22, 1988, p. 10.

24. "Sino-Soviet Trade," p. 40.

25. Ibid.; *Daily Report-China* (FBIS), October 21, 1988, p. 7.

26. "Sino-Soviet Trade," p. 42; *Daily Report-China* (FBIS), October 28, 1988, p. 6.

27. "Sino-Soviet Trade," p. 42; "Friendly Shopping Across the Border," *The Economist*, June 11, 1988, p. 35; "How Many Trees for a Computer?" *The Economist*, February 4, 1989, p. 33.

28. Strode, "Soviet China Policy," p. 345.

29. Mark D'Anastasio, "Soviets Now Hail China as a Source of Ideas for Reviving Socialism," *Wall Street Journal*, September 18, 1987, p. 1.

30. *Daily Report-Soviet Union* (FBIS), January 29, 1988, p. 16.

31. Cited by Strode, "Soviet China Policy," p. 345.

32. Ibid., p. 346.

33. *Daily Report-China* (FBIS), August 22, 1988, p. 4.

34. D'Anastasio, "Soviets Now Hail China," p. 8.

35. *Daily Report-China* (FBIS), June 1, 1988, p. 11.

36. Michael Kaser, "'One Economy, Two Systems': Parallels Between Soviet and Chinese Reform," *International Affairs* 63 (Summer 1987): 398.

37. Chi Su, "China and the Soviet Union: 'Principled, Salutary and Tempered' Management of Conflict," in *China and the World*, ed. Samuel S. Kim (Boulder, CO: Westview Press, 1984), pp. 149-150.

38. Cited by Strode, "Soviet China Policy," p. 334.

39. For an analysis of Gorbachev's speech, see Richard Nations, "Moscow's New Tack," *Far Eastern Economic Review*, August 14, 1986, pp. 30-34.

40. "Deng on Sino-Soviet, Sino-American Relations," *Beijing Review*, September 15, 1986, p. 5.

41. "A More Expansive, Relaxed, and Pragmatic Soviet World Outlook," translated in *China Report* (Joint Publication Research Service), July 15, 1987, pp. 1-3; the analysis parallels the points made by Stephen Sestanovich in "Gorbachev's Foreign Policy: A Diplomacy of Decline," *Problems of Communism* 37 (January-February 1988): 4.

42. *Daily Report-China* (FBIS), January 12, 1988, p. 5.

43. Strode, "Soviet China Policy," p. 335.

44. Ann Scott Tyson, "Sino-Soviet Talks Mark 'Common Ground' on Cambodia Conflict," *Christian Science Monitor*, September 2, 1988, p. 7.

45. Steven Erlanger, "Beijing Clarifies Position on Cambodia," *New York Times*, November 14, 1988, p. 3; for discussion of the benefits of full normalization, see articles from *Outlook* and *The World Economic Herald* in *Daily Report-China* (FBIS), October 12, 1988, pp. 9-10, and November 17, 1988, pp. 6-7, respectively.

46. A copy of the joint statements can be found in *Daily Report-China* (FBIS), February 6, 1989, pp. 16-17; the Japanese press report is noted in *Daily Report-China* (FBIS), February 13, 1989, p. 8.

47. Sestanovich, "Gorbachev's Foreign Policy," p. 6.

48. Marshall I. Goldman and Merle Goldman, "Soviet and Chinese Economic Reform," *Foreign Affairs* no. 3 (1987-88): 569.

49. For a discussion of the importance of these methods of political adaptation and the primacy of politics, see Stephen White, "Economic Performance and Communist Legitimacy," *World Politics* 3 (April 1986): 462-482.

50. Dobbs, "A Historic . . . Summit," p. 7.

51. Bill Keler, "Gorbachev Praises the Students and Declares Reform Is Necessary," *New York Times*, May 18, 1989, pp. 1 and 6.

CHAPTER 3

Cuba: Guarding the Revolution

JUAN M. del AGUILA

Attracted by the power of language, scholars and policy makers grapple with the new language emanating throughout the communist world, and place singular attention on perestroika and glasnost. These two terms, most directly associated with and articulated by Soviet President and Communist Party General Secretary Mikhail Gorbachev, resonate in the West and are interpreted to mean that a new generation of Soviet leaders is committed to profound structural change in the Soviet Union itself, and that the new language and its policy consequences will have an impact in other communist countries.

In its most pithy interpretation, perestroika is understood as the need to restructure a badly decayed Soviet economy, while glasnost is seen as an effort to gradually lift the veil of strict censorship and political conformity that has until recently governed how the Soviet government speaks to its citizens, and what they in return can freely express. A process of political reform that seeks to "democratize" the system by limiting the monolithic power of the Communist Party also aims to devolve a measure of power to local governments. National institutions like the Supreme Soviet are to become more autonomous from party control and exercise limited accountability on the political leadership, and vigorous criticism particularly of the government's performance is to be legitimated. The new language as well as the reforms under way presumably reflect "new thinking" in the Soviet Union, itself the product of a more realistic and pessimistic assessment by the Soviet leadership of what the foreseeable future holds for communism in the country.[1]

It is by now evident that changes under way in the Soviet Union are felt directly and indirectly in several other communist countries, principally in Eastern Europe. Still, it is difficult to determine the real impact of such changes or how deeply they are felt, how long such processes will last, or if they are ultimately desirable. The conventional wisdom in some scholarly circles maintains that communism is indeed receptive to new currents and that elites in communist countries finally realize that without new approaches communism is doomed to economic stagnation and political decay. Such an interpretation is partly wish fulfillment, insofar as personal desires invariably affect individual perceptions. The assumptions behind this reasoning are clearly that perestroika and glasnost are advancing and finding new converts in the communist world, and that it would be very difficult to turn the clock back and reverse them.

Yet is is also clear that resistance to perestroika and glasnost is found not only in the Soviet Union itself but also among its allies in Eastern Europe and Cuba. Entrenched elites in most communist countries fear an effective reduction in their power and privileged status as perestroika advances and moves political systems away from central control. If glasnost should ever institutionalize accountability, that would upset the political lines of command running from the top down in communist systems and question the "vanguard" role of ruling communist parties. In addition, Marxist-Leninist ideology is less essential to the new thinking than are values supportive of pragmatism and problem-solving, so that ideological erosion and "furious revisionism" are evident in the Soviet Union and other communist countries.

A mind-set that relies less on ideological distortions and more on rationality throws into question the raison d'être of Marxism-Leninism as the fountainhead of indisputable truths, and legitimates independent thinking and critical inquiry. Since communist regimes like Cuba's discourage and often punish manifestations of public criticism and maintain strict limits on what is or is not permissible conduct, any systematic challenge to core ideological beliefs is bound to be perceived officially as a threat.

In this chapter, I will examine what impact—if any—Soviet-style perestroika (*re-estructuración*) and glasnost (*apertura* or *transparencia*) are having in Cuba and how the Cuban regime is reacting to these changes. One need not assume that the regime accepts the common interpretation of either process in order to adapt them to Cuba's reality, because the meaning of ideas is always subject to official definitions and specific understandings. Consequently, the basic premise is that Cuba is neither subordinated to the Soviet understanding of perestroika and glasnost, nor a completely isolated actor that can shut out Soviet suggestions and reject "new thinking" altogether. Rather, Cuba is effectively a Soviet client state quite able to maintain internal political autonomy and it has the means, will, and experience either to redefine perestroika and glasnost in its own terms or reject them altogether.

THE NEW CUBAN CONTEXT

The protracted succession crisis in the Soviet Union in the early 1980s and the eventual emergence of Mikhail Gorbachev as Communist Party general secretary and subsequently as de facto president and head of state forced the Cuban regime to deal with new realities. Familiar relationships sustained with the Brezhnev regime were strained as new personalities rose to influential positions under Gorbachev, many of whom were younger technocrats unfamiliar with Cuba and its problems. In addition, for the first time President Castro faced a younger Soviet leader, one who did not necessarily share the somewhat paternalistic outlook of his predecessors toward Cuba and its leader, and had no reason to believe that Cuba should maintain its relatively privileged status among Soviet clients in the Third World. Neither Gorbachev nor any of his top advisors and colleagues placed Cuba's agenda higher than that of other communist countries, and during the last few years the new Soviet regime has clearly focused much of its energy on domestic issues.

Soviet foreign policy initiatives have been aimed at improving relations with the United States and Western Europe, at finding a face-saving withdrawal from Afghanistan, at shaking up the ossified mentality and rigid bureaucracies of Moscow's East European allies, and at reaching a rapprochement with the People's Republic of China. Some analysts contend that Moscow's behavior is the product of a "conceptual revolution" whose national security and strategic consequences are evident. From this perspective, Marxism-Leninism no longer provides the dominant framework for policy makers, so the belief in "the international class struggle" is nearly obsolete. Of particular significance is the fact that Moscow's introspection leads it to reject its "revolutionary faith" in the prospects of political change in the Third World, so that support for wars of national liberation or regional struggles is no longer central to Kremlin policy makers. Indeed, Robert Levgold argues that "Third World conflicts are portrayed as a vast drain on the pitiful resources of developing countries," no longer viewed as part of an inevitable historical struggle between capitalism and communism.[2]

Havana takes an entirely different perspective on the meaning and desirability of perestroika and glasnost. Its view is shaped by its Third World role, its belief in revolutionary struggles in the developing world, a pervasive and often useful sense of insecurity, and not in the least by President Castro's deep-seated revolutionary convictions. In other words, Havana takes itself to be "a paladin of the oppressed" in the Third World, even if Moscow is gradually pulling back from commitments to pro-Soviet regimes and groups. In addition, Cuba must be an example to its friends and remain as a loyal advocate of Third World causes, calling either for an international redistribution of wealth, or for a moratorium on external debt for Latin American countries. Finally, Cuba considers itself an always-vulnerable outpost of the communist world next to the imperialist superpower, and an ever-defiant regime that refuses to compromise its Marxist-Leininst principles precisely because others are questioning theirs.

In its political development, Cuba has at times introduced Soviet-induced reforms, but in other instances has followed its own designs. The adoption of the now-discredited System of Economic Management and Planning (SPDE) in the late 1970s meant that the regime experimented with market mechanisms and material incentives without abolishing central planning. In the 1980s, the leadership reversed itself on the grounds that the emphasis on mechanisms overlooked the need for constant political work, and created a destructive "consumerist mentality." President Castro had approved of SPDE, but eventually reversed himself on the grounds that "mechanisms must be auxiliary means to the work of man, of political and revolutionary work; otherwise it would be impossible to build socialism."[3] The primacy of politics over economics is clearly restated.

There is much evidence (and Castro's past behavior) to suggest that the need to reaffirm socialism's legitimacy at the time when its very ideological foundation is under intense questioning is what leads President Castro to pronounce his (and Havana's) absolute faith in it, trumping the revisionists in the communist world. For example, speaking at the 35th anniversary of the attack on the Moncada barracks, President Castro stated:

> We believe in socialism, and we therefore have to be very careful in interpreting and application of the theory, we have to be very careful in each step that we take. And the Revolution was always like that, and now the child is 30 years old and he is healthy, robust, strong, only 90 miles away from the United States.[4]

It is thus clear that to the Cuban regime, socialism is a defense mechanism, a barrier that protects the nation against capitalist penetration. Consequently, it should not be diluted in difficult times.

On the other hand, if socialism and the revolution were as strong and healthy as the president proclaims, there would be little need to reaffirm their merits constantly, nor would there be any reason to carp on the evident deficiencies of the Cuban system. Indeed, the president himself has repeatedly pointed out just how difficult the internal situation is, and has indicated that "whatever is wrong here, is our fault, yours and ours, of each worker in his workplace and of each supervisor."[5] Moreover, Castro regularly scolds the masses, workers, and administrators for ideological laxity, for not paying sufficient attention to political work, and for wallowing in social indiscipline. In his own words:

> What is done badly, incorrectly, shoddy things, negligence, social indiscipline, including delinquency, are in the ideological area like barges that can approach our coasts to invade our territories. . . . We fight against objective and material difficulties and try to defeat them. The battle is not easy. Difficulties may increase, indeed: we are in a special situation.[6]

Evidently the society finds itself in a multilayered crisis affecting not only economic performance, but more importantly basic values and attitudes. Still, the regime refuses to recognize that the political, social, and cultural straitjacket imposed by orthodox socialism sustains the very crisis in which Cuba finds itself, and that laxity, indolence, and political disaffection are symptoms of a much deeper national crisis.

The Cuban regime rejects the notion that the crisis stems from the accumulated grievances layered into the system during 30 years of revolution and social experimentation. It admits that building socialism is extremely difficult and that "mistakes have been committed," but it does not question the legitimacy of the initial decisions to move ahead with a project of revolutionary socialism. Debate on this question is closed, and there is no room for revisionist approaches. Individuals and many in positions of leadership have at times abused power, but that is seen as the result of personal deficiencies or human frailties. In short, unlike some of the more spirited Soviet revisionists who now question the essence of the Soviet revolution itself and may yet take on Lenin and his legacy, the Cubans are not about to strip away useful revolutionary mythology.

On the other hand, Havana prides itself in going its own way at times or, in the current parlance, "build socialism in the correct way." The Campaign of Rectification of Errors and Negative Tendencies launched in 1984–85 aims to restore communist militancy and ideological zeal to a society showing measurable signs of disaffection and discontent, generated partly by permanent austerity and by the realization that the future is not promising. President Castro believes that more socialist measures are necessary in order to resolve current problems, and that economic and political liberalization are unnecessary. Indeed, he categorically rules out either political reform or the return to market instruments, because such practices are completely worthless, with their emphasis on vulgar politics (*politiquería incesante*). Castro's hostility to anything that smacks of capitalism and a market economy is visceral, because to him that means only materialism, consumerism, profiteering, and selfishness. It is an outmoded and simplistic view that practitioners of socialism elsewhere are furiously rejecting.

At the same time, declining growth rates and a severe shortage of hard currency adversely affect consumer demand and restrict imports, while little genuine economic diversification has taken place. Major deficiencies in the highly centralized command model are the result of episodic conflicts between ideology and pragmatism, and these produce erratic economic goals and lend themselves to abrupt policy turns.[7] The Campaign of Rectification has yet to rectify adverse economic trends and produce tangible payoffs, and it is not clear that the "negative tendencies" it is designed to reverse have been uprooted. In the end, the regime candidly admits that the next several years will be the most difficult.

Appeals to sacrifice and conscience indicate that Guevarist doctrines are rediscovered, and the rhetoric of the New Man is once again pervasive. Without the proper attitude, President Castro contends, socialism cannot be achieved nor communism reached. Selflessness, altruism, and voluntarism are once again encouraged. For instance, micro-brigades have been reorganized and put to work in construction, sanitation, and clean-ups, and those workers are held up as examples. Special contingents carry out specific social tasks, such as building houses and day care centers. These are considered innovations in labor management methods, a unique Cuban contribution to the building of socialism. The work of these special contingents is adversely affected by critical shortages in construction and other materials, so that manpower is at times wasted due to supply problems. Still, the emphasis on labor discipline is essential as is the willingness to sacrifice and go the extra mile at a time when resources are very tight and the international situation unfavorable.

The Campaign of Rectification is in fact a moral crusade designed to uproot antisocialist attitudes found among technocrats, managers, administrators, and Communist Party cadres. Hundreds have been purged as a result of deficiencies in their work, and party cadres in particular are constantly reminded of the obligations of a loyal communist. The Campaign harks back to the Revolutionary Offensive of the late 1960s, when the regime decreed the complete nationalization of small-scale private commerce and production. Guevara had argued that socialism is incompatible with acquisitive and profit-oriented attitudes, and that view shaped the return to moralism and the abolition of peasant free markets in the 1980s.

President Castro has severely criticized "corrupting" influences stemming from speculation and profiteering, blaming the advocates of the SPDE for introducing capitalist mechanisms in order to improve economic efficiency. Humberto Perez, its principal advocate, lost his position as director of the Central Planning Agency in a major bureaucratic reshuffling in 1986, and many of his former collaborators suffered the same fate. President Castro approved of the SPDE in the late 1970s and seemed to be swayed by the logic of efficiency for several years, but he abruptly reversed the policy in 1984 and is held blameless. This is a recurring feature of the Cuban system, namely the complete lack of accountability of President Castro in particular and most top policy makers in general.

In addition, values antithetical to communism are found among the masses, suggesting that socialization efforts have failed to instill the proper mentality in many members of the revolutionary generation. In the same Moncada anniversary speech, Castro continued to denigrate the advocates of market reforms as well as those with "petit bourgeois opinions" and he categorically stated that "what I can tell the imperialists and the theorists of imperialism is that Cuba will never adopt methods, styles, philosophies nor idiosyncracies of capitalism. That I can say!"[8]

The Communist Party itself is aware of flagging discipline and waning zeal among its own cadres as well as the masses, and it seeks to "eradicate with energy the manifestations of indolence and negligent attitudes, alien to the essence of socialism and the Revolution's policies." In fact, the party points to "examples of public opinion that reflect uncertainties, worries and manifestations of incomprehension and irritability," so that real grievances are at the root of many social problems. Finally, the party urges the masses to deepen their commitment to building socialism, but it recognizes "manifestations of social and labor indiscipline in some individuals' behavior."[9]

It is thus quite clear that appeals to "socialist consciousness" have so far failed to motivate many workers to produce more, administrators and technocrats to improve management, or even party cadres to take their responsibilities seriously. The regime is on the defensive in the ideological front, but its strategy is to batten down the hatches, reaffirm the need for ideological purity, and reintroduce appeals to consciousness, sacrifice, and patriotism. Its view is that difficulties can be overcome according to Cuba's "own realities and conceptions," indicating its refusal to promote internal reforms for their own sake.

As was the case when medieval monks preserved Catholicism against pagan doctrines, Cuba's ideologues seek to invigorate Marxism-Leninism against foreign and domestic heretics. A theory whose failures are evident not only in the communist world but also in underdeveloped societies like Nicaragua, Angola, and elsewhere is revived in Cuba at a time when regional if not global trends threaten to dismiss it altogether as an organizing principle. The country could well become the communist world's monastery in the late twentieth century, an isolated shrine in a world besieged by ideological confusion.

President Castro appears to be one of the last true believers in Marxist-Leninist ideology, and he remains a most recalcitrant ruler opposed to substantive economic reform or limited political liberalization. For the Cuban president, perestroika and glasnost represent a crass betrayal of communism itself, an explicit repudiation of centralized political control and a rejection of class struggle as one of communism's basic laws. Influenced by Guevarist doctrines and by the thought of radical utopians, the president's absolutist convictions stand out in the communist world's ideological disarray. For Fidel Castro, compromises with capitalism and imperialism may be tactically necessary, but should never lead one to repudiate basic principles, or believe that one can reform communism with capitalist methods. Against revisionism and liberalization one should always maintain "revolutionary intransigence and loyalty to principles," because to do otherwise signals retreat and, eventually, defeat.

Finally, Gorbachev's warning that "perestroika and glasnost represent the Soviet Union's last opportunity" to become a developed society stands as clear evidence of Moscow's ideological abdication, and of its renunciation of basic communist principles. In contrast, Cuba once again proclaims its unswerving commitment to communism, or as Castro himself declares:

Today, 30 years after that January 1, we can assure you that our people will always be loyal to the principles of socialism! That our people will always be loyal to the principles of Marxism-Leninism! That our people will always be loyal to the principles of internationalism![10]

In sum, the fact that the process of questioning socialism and communism comes from the Soviet Union, long portrayed as the motherland of all communists and as the society that had set for itself the task of full human development, does not mean that Cuba must follow the same path. Rather, it must remain wedded to orthodoxy at all costs, perhaps waiting for perestroika to fail and for Moscow's return to its senses.

Fundamental political reforms in Cuba have also been ruled out. The Communist Party's monopoly on power is not to be challenged, and the party itself will continue to lead the process of building socialism. A key aim of the Campaign of Rectification is to strengthen the work of the party and extend its authority over the workings of local and provincial governments. The party is the vanguard, its elite character and central role must be maintained.

Finally, talk of democratization at the grass roots is likewise foolish, because the Cuban government believes that its system is one of the most democratic in the world. Cuban-style democracy is characterized by elections at the local level to the Organs of Peoples

Power, and these local bodies subsequently choose provincial and national legislators. The Communist Party closely monitors the nomination and election process, though not everyone elected to local office need be a party member.

On the other hand, there is no competition among candidates, most of them have the "correct" political attitudes, and by the time the National Assembly is chosen, practically all of its members belong to the Communist Party. The National Assembly itself is a captive institution that routinely approves what the top political leadership submits to it. Its votes are most often unanimous and it has never challenged the leadership's policies. It is not an independent institution, nor are its members really accountable to either the provincial or local assemblies that elected them.

To think of democratic elections in one-party states is to distort reality beyond comprehension, and the Marxist-Leninist definition of democracy is not remotely connected to most scholars' understanding of the term. In any event, the Cuban system does not need reform because President Castro maintains that it is much more democratic than capitalist countries. In this as in all key matters of domestic policy, the president's word is final and if others in the top political elite either disagree with him or see the need to gradually liberalize the polity, they fail to speak out.

In conclusion, the Cuban government sees no need to restructure either the economy or the polity through measures similar to those being enacted in other communist countries. Privatization of commerce, agriculture, or industry is ruled out, so that for all practical purposes the state remains as the only producer and employer. The idea of profit and gain is attacked and delegitimated, held to be incompatible with socialism. Political reforms are not contemplated, and the Communist Party neither practices internal democracy nor faces a dilution of its authority. Without its leading role, genuine socialism cannot be built.

INTERNAL CHANGES AND SIGNS OF POTENTIAL CLEAVAGES

The most serious dilemma facing the Cuban regime stems from its refusal to relax ideological rigor at the time when its principal allies rapidly do so, and from its failure to liberalize the polity. As the ideological fountainhead for Cuban communism, President Castro's explicit rejection of "alien" practices and his insistence that the nation follow its own "realities and experiences" makes him the leader of the most conservative camp, but there is growing evidence that pro-reform factions exist in the top political elite.

In his critical speeches, the president uses the harshest language against "small time imitators and copiers" (*copiadores e imitadores de pacotilla*) advocating that Cuba imitate what is done elsewhere. Portraying them as weak and ignorant of just how different Cuba is from other socialist countries, he scornfully points to

> some who believe that what others are doing is what we must immediately do; there are also brains like those, people without self-confidence, without confidence in their homeland, without confidence in their people, without confidence in their Revolution, that immediately say that we have to copy. That is an incorrect attitude, an erroneous attitude, because... some have some problems, others have different problems; some commit some mistakes, others make different mistakes.[11]

Finally, Castro is not shy about his own personal convictions, and reminds his listeners that "I have nothing but contempt for those who let themselves be carried away by foolishness and illusions, for those who are weak of heart, weak of mind, weak of will, incapable of understanding these realities."

Without explicitly saying so, it is clear that the president knows that pro-reform elements are present in the party, government, and quite probably in key administrative and managerial positions. Their knowledge of how the economy functions and their hands-on experience with pressing economic problems may well be the reason for their pro-reform attitudes. Since 1986, the political leadership has been removing many potential reformers from important positions, and sanctioning and reprimanding others.[12]

One can safely assume that advocates of reform are also found in the armed forces, though it would be fatal for any officer to identify himself publicly with anti-Castro factions. One of the essential characteristics of the Cuban system under Castro has been supreme loyalty to the president, so that evident signs of disagreement are quickly turned into questions of personal disloyalty to the commander in chief. This pattern continues to hold, because the president is laying down the line to overt and covert reformers, labeling them as poor revolutionaries that lack the will and discipline necessary to overcome the present crisis. For the president, true revolutionaries remain until the bitter end, and show their mettle precisely when objective and subjective conditions are most difficult.

In sum, the very fact that President Castro has been so outspoken and unequivocal in his opposition to meaningful reforms demonstrates that there is growing discontent within the regime, and that the carefully crafted image of unity can no longer be sustained. Using a variety of fora such as anniversaries, special meetings, and even casual reunions to deliver his profoundly orthodox message also indicates that Castro feels the need to restate his antiperestroika views as often as possible, so that the basic themes remain undiluted. Chastising and scolding from the top, the president is clearly placing his prestige on the line against reformist elements.

All of this indicates that the struggle *within* the regime is far from over, and that the debate has taken on some apocalyptic pronouncements regarding the very future of Cuban socialism. Purges, dismissals, and shifts in the top organs of the party and the government mean that the president and his unconditional allies can enforce orthodoxy, but at what is clearly an escalating cost. In a very ironic sense, the cultural norm of *obedezco pero no cumplo* (I obey but I do not comply), thought to be obsolete under socialism, may well be a source of internal resistance. It is impossible to determine how strong these pro-reform groups are—or who their leaders might be—but it is clear that their advocacy is perceived as a major threat by President Castro and the orthodox faction.

On the other hand, there is a growing body of evidence indicating that forces in "civil society" are increasingly active, often working through an informal network of associations articulating human rights themes. For example, several dissident organizations exist and some have attracted international attention. Among these, one finds the Cuban Committee for Human Rights, the Martiano Committee for Human Rights, the Cuban Commission of Human Rights and National Reconciliation, and the small Party on Behalf of Human Rights.[13] Established organizations like Amnesty International, Americas Watch, and the United Nations Commission of Human Rights know of the Cuban organizations, and recognize them as legitimate and competent entities. Their spokespersons maintain contact with their counterparts in the United States, and, on occasion, someone is allowed to travel abroad.

On the other hand, these Cuban groups do not operate legally nor are they viewed as legitimate popular organizations by the Cuban government. Still, their existence is clear proof of limited antiregime organizational activity, and of an underground democratic political subculture that has survived in a hostile environment. It is impossible to determine whether the values of this subculture reject socialism as such, or only its blatantly dictatorial practices under the Castro regime. There is reason to believe that members of unofficial groups are influenced by European and Latin American social democratic ideas, and are not necessarily sympathetic to democratic capitalism. Others clearly reject Marxism-Leninism but do so from a nationalistic and antiimperialist posture, looking to the teachings of José Marti for their inspiration. In sum, an incipient and still isolated network of democratic organizations has surfaced after 30 years of monolithic totalitarianism, but its status is precarious and its social impact still negligible.

The international community is increasingly aware of past and present human rights violations in Cuba, and the view that its brand of revolutionary socialism was (and is) benign is less and less credible. Personal testimonials, official investigations from the Organization of American States and private organizations, inquiries by the U.S. Congress, and powerful books like Armando Valladares' *Against All Hope* ripped open the regime's "humanistic" claims and provided irrefutable evidence of official repression and brutality.

For political and ideological reasons, Cuba was able to stop inquiries by international organizations into its internal affairs for nearly three decades, but in recent years the UN Commission on Human Rights, the International Red Cross, and Americas Watch itself have sent delegations to Cuba and conducted independent investigations. Over time, this could strengthen the work of the Cuban organizations and further legitimate their standing abroad.

For instance, the government permitted inspections by Amnesty International and the New York City Bar Association in 1988, but it strongly defends its human rights practices, particularly against U.S. charges of possible violations. Observers were allowed to visit prisoners in jails, and to recommend that the government adhere to international norms covering the treatment of prisoners. The UN Human Rights Commission sent its own delegation in 1988, and received numerous complaints from individual citizens. Its subsequent report noted the absence of civil and political liberties, pervasive censorship over the communications media, and degrading treatment of prisoners in the past.

The number of political prisoners has dwindled to a few hundred in recent years, and there is evidence to the effect that the worst abuses are a thing of the past. The U.S. State Department holds that prison conditions have improved, and reform of the Penal Code has decriminalized petty offenses that had previously been judged as political. These are positive changes that stem from both international pressure and governmental decision, but conventional civil and political rights do not exist. The regime is clearly on the defensive on the larger question of human rights and President Castro himself reportedly becomes very angry when the issue is raised in private conversations with foreigners interested in the matter. In his mind and officially, human rights are fully protected in Cuba.

The Cuban Committee for Human Rights has at times been mired in controversy and plagued by personal rivalries among its founders and members, so that its effectiveness is limited not only by the hostile environment in Cuba itself but by internecine quarrels as well. It patterns itself after groups of dissident intellectuals in Eastern Europe and the Soviet Union, and its principal purpose is to point out specific cases of human rights violations in Cuban prisons and other places. In addition, the Committee has staged protests, circulated dissident material, denounced human rights abuses, and established ties with human rights organizations abroad. Retribution has at times come swiftly, and its leaders have been constantly harassed by Cuban authorities. Some of them have gone to prison as a consequence of their activities, most of which are illegal under Cuban law.[14]

The existence of these organizations in Cuba shatters the myth of national unity so cherished by the regime. All of these are in one way or another "dissident" organizations that question both Marxist-Leninist ideology and the explicit limitations on basic rights and freedoms found in the 1976 Constitution. Some of the bolder leaders, like Samuel Martinez Lara of the Party for Human Rights, appeared on CBS television during President Gorbachev's visit to Cuba and called for a plebiscite with or without President Castro's approval. He and others were subsequently arrested and fined, but it is the first time in my memory that someone *in* Cuba publicly and so openly challenged the system and its leaders to a foreign audience.

Dissidence is prohibited under Cuban law, but the law itself is the product of Leninist ideology and is not designed to protect individuals in political disputes with the government. Legal scholars of communist systems often point to the nature of law itself as a fundamental impediment in the exercise of individual rights, so that dissent is not protected under law and it does not treat dissent as legitimate. "Illegal conduct" is interpreted very broadly in Cuba, so that the legal system does not afford redress for political grievances but in fact judges them arbitrarily. One of the founders of the Cuban Committee for Human Rights explains that

> the Constitution says that none of the freedoms it grants, can be used to criticize the social system, that is, socialism, and therefore the government. This is something ironic. The Constitution, in fact the government of Cuba, guarantees liberty to those people who support it, but not liberty in its most fundamental sense: the right to oppose without being suppressed.... Therefore, the creation of organizations such as our committee, is, to a certain degree, precluded by constitutional spirit.... The problem, then, is fundamentally a constitutional issue.[15]

In sum, the constitutional conundrum remains unresolved and is specifically designed to maintain the political monopoly of ruling communist parties. The Cuban constitution of 1976 is by design an exclusionary document, because it recognizes only the existence of pro-regime organizations. By ruling out political reforms, the regime is also rejecting the kinds of legal reforms that might countenance "unofficial pluralism," so that human rights organizations exist in limbo and their members are subject to harassment and social vilification.

Finally, only revolutionary mass organizations like the Committees for Defense of the Revolution, the Communist Youth Union, or the Cuban Women's Federation are sanctioned, so that the legal system cannot offer protection to nongovernmental bodies. These organizations are controlled from above and their objectives are in line with those approved of by the regime, so they do not have an independent political life. Cuba's government places a premium on internal unity, and group behavior is conditioned by the premise. Consequently, nonofficial bodies cannot be legalized and protected because the constitutional framework is consciously set up to exclude them and because organizational unity is one of the supreme values of the political culture. Stepping out of that framework brings retribution, isolation, and the label of being an "antiregime organization."

In conclusion, the political system remains unchanged with the Communist Party still in full control. In their advocacy of orthodoxy,

President Castro and others in the top political elite do face some resistance, particularly from younger cadres, but no institutional cleavages have emerged. Factions exist in the Central Committee and probably inside the state bureaucracy, but it is impossible to determine their strength or what if any substantive policy differences these groups may have with the top leadership. If there are challengers waiting in the wings, their status is extremely risky and any manifestation of disloyalty would prove to be politically fatal.

Marxist-Leninist ideology shapes officialdom, but there is reason to believe that its influence on society is markedly declining and that it may face secular challenges. Its power as a galvanizing and mobilizing force is practically gone, though there is no group or institution articulating a "counterideology." Criticism of the regime, the party, or the top leadership is suppressed and dissent is prohibited. Complaints about the quality of goods, services, or workmanship are tolerated and even encouraged, and blame is now laid on workers, managers, and administrators.

Finally, there is no independent political life to speak of outside of the mass organizations, and their behavior is docile and supportive of the regime. Organized labor is controlled from above and workers do not have the right to strike or bargain independently. Neither religious, ethnic, nor regional cleavages nourish antiregime forces. Several unofficial groups have established a precarious presence and form an informal associational network, but they have no legal standing and their activities are severely limited. Depending on circumstances, the regime either tolerates or represses them.

GORBACHEV'S VISIT AND ITS CONSEQUENCES

The long-awaited visit to Cuba of Soviet President Mikhail Gorbachev finally took place during April 1989. Most of the Cuban media had been downplaying the reforms taking place in the Soviet Union and other parts of the communist world, emphasizing the differences between Cuba and other communist countries. Havana emphasizes its "own path to building socialism," and sees no reason to repeat the mistakes that others have made. In other words, the Cuban government makes it clear that domestic politics are its business, and that it can and often should reject friendly advice. Moscow recognizes the propriety of leaving "internal affairs" untouched, but it is clear that it prefers to see changes in how the Cuban economy is managed.

In addition, Mr. Gorbachev's insistence on further improvement in East-West relations did not bring him the recognition that might have been expected from a Soviet client, partly because Havana fears that Moscow has shamefully abdicated to the capitalist world. The Cuban government is skeptical about the new rapprochement between the superpowers, and is driven by the belief that Cuba remains vulnerable and perhaps increasingly isolated because of it. For instance, there is no doubt that Cuba disagreed with the Soviet withdrawal from Afghanistan and viewed it as a shameful defeat for socialism. It resented Moscow's urgings on the need for a settlement in southern Africa, so that socialism did not triumph there either. In sum, the Cuban government has probably reached the conclusion that Moscow's staying power in seeing revolutionary conflicts through to the end is considerably diluted, and there is no question that President Gorbachev has been instrumental in bringing it about.

Personal comparisons between an appealing Soviet leader dressed in expensive suits and President Castro, who personifies the image of the fading caudillo often found in Gabriel García Márquez's novels, are indicative of the divergent paths that Cuba and the Soviet Union are taking. Gorbachev is viewed as an aggressive modernizer who has rationally determined that the systemic crisis affecting the Soviet Union must be vigorously addressed with clear thinking, market-driven incentives, and political reforms. On the other hand, President Castro suits up in military garb, reaffirms an increasingly outmoded orthodoxy, rejects political and economic reforms, and rules out criticism of the system, of communism, or of his omniscient and omnipresent role. The more things change abroad, the more they stay the same in Cuba.

Changes under way in the communist world will gradually isolate Cuba from the Soviet Union and other communist countries, because Cuba's approach emphasizes centralization, nonmarket instruments, moral stimuli, and political rectitude. This path failed precipitately in the 1960s and going into the 1990s the society is wearier, more cynical, and less willing to believe in the "future of socialism" than was the case during the revolution's first years. Social fatigue and political disillusionment, not revolutionary commitment and a sense of "being on the right side of history," characterize basic attitudes.

Despite government efforts to censor reports of what is happening in parts of the communist world, information about it reaches the public via the Voice of America's Radio Marti and other outlets. In all likelihood, Cubans know of the turmoil in the Baltic and other Soviet republics, of Solidarity's success in Poland, of popular repudiation of ruling communist parties in Eastern Europe and of Gorbachev's popularity in the West. It is impossible to determine what impact this information has on the political elite or on sophisticated technocrats and other policy makers, but there is no doubt that comparisons between the situation in Cuba and transformations under way in the communist world force individuals to rethink just why the Cuban system is stuck and where it is headed.

A curious role-reversal has occurred, namely that Cuba is now perceived as sclerotic and irrelevant, while other communist countries are moving away from totalitarianism through limited liberalization. Nationalism and antiimperialism have shaped the Cuban revolutionary process in a fundamental way, and have been manipulated to preserve a strong sense of unity and defiance. Yet the communications and technological revolutions spill over national barriers and official truths lose their legitimacy as more and more information about the outside world penetrates the country. As new currents sweep the communist world and Soviet-style communism faces up to a grim legacy of brutality, corruption, and alienation, the Cuban regime attempts to shut out "harmful" influences and genuine democratic ideas.

In his speech to Cuba's National Assembly, President Gorbachev made it plain that Soviet foreign policy is moving away from supporting revolutionary movements in the Third World, despite the fact that Moscow is still engaged in Central America, Africa, and other regions. As a practical matter, Moscow cannot completely disengage from the Third World nor unilaterally forfeit its competition with the United States, but it is refocusing its aims on Europe and on the nuclear and strategic fronts. For instance, the ideological justification for "armed struggle" has been practically discarded, and it is increasingly evident that Moscow no longer views the world as divided between two irreconcilable camps. Deemphasizing Marxist-Leninist verities in favor of realism and pragmatism in international relations is not only a sign of ideological decay, but also a clear signal from Moscow to Havana on the usefulness of radical adventurism.[16]

On the other hand, it is not clear that Moscow is pressuring Havana into a partial disengagement from regional trouble spots like

Central America, or that the Kremlin is prepared to dramatically curtail its economic and technical assistance to Cuba in order to moderate its foreign intrusions. Soviet spokespersons mention the need to "balance the economic ties" between Cuba and the Soviet Union, but given the structural asymmetries between these trade partners that is not a realistic outlook. In fact, if the Soviets pushed for such a balance, the impact on Cuba's economy would be devastating because it could be achieved only through a severe contraction of Soviet assistance.[17]

Total Soviet assistance to Cuba runs to some $6 billion per year, and that is nearly 50 percent of Moscow's total foreign aid. In the last 25 years or so, Cuba has accumulated a total debt to the Soviet Union of well above $20 billion, so Moscow's underwriting of its Cuban client has not come cheap. Cuba's debt to the Soviet Union was first due in 1972 and then pushed forward to 1986, and at that point it was again rescheduled until 1991. There were expectations in Cuba regarding the cancellation of either part or all of this debt, but Gorbachev failed to write it off. The prospects that Cuba can or will repay even a small portion of this enormous debt are dubious, and the Soviet Union is probably resigned to that.

Havana's proletarian internationalism is the very antithesis of Moscow's "new thinking," but a vigorous assertion of internationalism is a core principle in Cuban foreign policy. During a press conference in Havana with President Gorbachev at his side, President Castro stated that "the Soviet Union and the United States have nothing to say about Cuba's foreign relations,"[18] which could be seen as a typical *fidelista* boast or as a sharp reminder to Moscow of its limited influence over Havana's conduct. In any case, Havana is once again playing the maverick of the communist world, defying not only its traditional antagonist, the United States, but an accommodationist Soviet Union as well.

At the end of the April 1989 summit, Cuba and the Soviet Union signed a 25-year Treaty of Friendship that restates the general conditions of "fraternal cooperation" without mentioning the growing divergence in each country's view of the future. For Moscow, Cuba remains as an unproductive client with little prospect of sustaining itself without massive subsidies and technical inputs, so that it will continue to need a disproportionate amount of Moscow's foreign assistance. Cuba's value as a strategic asset reduces the likelihood that the Soviet Union will gradually cut it loose, but there is no doubt that Cuban-Soviet relations are entering a period of strain and political estrangement rather than one in which the client continues to act in concert with the sponsor.

Assessments of the consequences of President Gorbachev's visit to Cuba are varied. On the one hand, some view the visit as a watershed event in which the Soviet leader granted his blessing to the most faithful of Moscow's revolutionary clients, and at the same time reminded his hosts that old approaches are increasingly irrelevant in a changing global environment. From his position, Gorbachev looks at the world with an East-West perspective that gives him entry into "the club" and is not shared in Havana, where vulnerability is politically sacrosanct.

A second interpretation maintains that the meeting between a reformist Soviet leader and an unrepentant radical like President Castro simply showed the two faces of communism in the late twentieth century, namely the kind that would collapse rapidly without major restructuring, and the type that will stagnate for the foreseeable future. Gorbachev is thus struggling against a systemic calamity, but Castro is convinced that his creation will be revived and eventually flourish. It is clear that Gorbachev's apocalyptic vision regarding the Soviet Union's "last opportunity" to become an advanced society reflects a more realistic appraisal of his country's problems than Castro's belief that the revolution will "live to be 50, 60, and 100 years," but Gorbachev is not a boastful man.[19]

Finally, the aftermath of the Soviet leader's visit may not adversely affect the institutionalized agenda between Cuba and the Soviet Union in the short run given the real interests between the two, but it is unlikely that Cuba will retain its privileged place among Moscow's Third World clients. In other words, Soviet leverage over Cuban behavior is limited and Cuba's ability to shift away from Moscow is constrained by its dependence on it. Viewing President Castro as an incorrigible "problem child," a new generation of Soviet leaders can put up with Havana's independence until Cuba's revolutionary flames are suffocated either by internal changes or repeated failures abroad. At that point, Moscow can seriously deemphasize its ties and "fraternal obligations" to Havana and wonder whether the enterprise really did pay off.

CONCLUSION

The Cuban political system remains a one-party regime dominated by practically the same revolutionary elite that came to power in 1959. It has consciously rejected perestroika and glasnost on the grounds that national peculiarities make reform unnecessary, and because Cuba must stand on its uniqueness. At a time when ideological confusion afflicts the communist world, Cuba reaffirms its unyielding faith in Marxism-Leninism, and President Castro calls for a new spirit of revolutionary consciousness.

The dominant values in the political culture emphasize unity in the face of adversity and national will against the imperialist menace, but the evidence presented here suggests that an incipient democratic subculture rejects much of the collectivist ethos. The notion of individual rights persists in a hostile environment, though it is not grounded in the social milieu. The subordination of official organization to regime goals means that "civil society" remains passive, led by neither the intelligentsia nor any antisystem faction. In fact, the Cuban intelligentsia is characterized by intellectual sterility and political docility, and its product is profoundly conservative. Its cultural rituals are uncritical and self-congratulatory, always reaffirming unswerving loyalty to the system and its leader.

A controlled mass media dilutes the impact of "new currents" slowly reshaping communist societies elsewhere, but uncensored information does reach the public. One cannot assume that individuals will conclude that changes abroad are healthy and might be applicable to Cuba, but the society cannot isolate itself from powerful trends elsewhere. In time, new ideas may justify an entirely new path, produce a genuine intellectual reawakening, and shake up the country's cultural foundation.

Finally, difficulties and estrangement, rather than a harmony of views or successful geopolitical cooperation, are bound to strain Cuban-Soviet relations. A revolutionary state convinced of its historical mission is bound to create difficulties for a superpower that no longer speaks in universal terms and is rapidly shifting its focus from external adventurism to internal rebuilding. Cuba could find itself as an outcast in the communist world before it can rebuild its ties in Latin America or entice the United States into normalizing relations with it, so that its regime is faced with unprecedented challenges abroad. In the end, for Cuba revolution is everything, for the Soviets and the Latin Americans it is becoming incidental.

NOTES

1. Gorbachev's views appear in his *Perestroika* (New York: Harper and Row, 1987). Additional sources are Abel Aganbeygan, *The Challenge: Economics of Perestroika* (London: Hutchinson, 1988); Seweryn Bialer and Michael Mendelbaum, eds. *Gorbachev's Russia and American Foreign Policy* (Boulder, CO: Westview Press, 1988).

2. Robert Levgold, "The Revolution in Soviet Foreign Policy," *Foreign Affairs: America and the World* 68 (1988-89): 86.

3. Fidel Castro, *Por el Camino Correcto* (Havana: Editora Política, 1987), p. 80.

4. President Castro's speech, December 5, 1988, *Granma Resumen Semanal*, December 18, 1988.

5. Ibid.

6. Ibid.

7. See the chapter by Carmelo Mesa-Lago, "The Cuban Economy in the 1980s: The Return of Ideology," in *Socialist Cuba, Past Interpretations and Future Challenges*, ed. Sergio Roca (Boulder, CO: Westview Press, 1988), pp. 59-100; "Drought and Weak Oil Prices Lead to Slump in Cuban Economy," *Latin America Weekly Report*, July 14, 1988; "Castro Warns of Further Belt Tightening," *Caribbean Report*, February 25, 1988.

8. *Granma Resumen Semanal*, December 12, 1988.

9. "Analizan el Buro Político y el Secretariado Cambios Positivos e Insuficiencias en la Situación del Pais," *Gramma Resumen Semanal*, October 2, 1988.

10. President Castro's speech, January 1, 1989. *Granma Resumen Semanal*, January 15, 1989.

11. President Castro's speech, July 26, 1988, *Granma Resumen Semanal*, August 7, 1988.

12. "PCC Told to Deal with Criticism," *Latin America Weekly Report*, December 11, 1986; "Purga masiva en La Habana," *El Neuvo Herald*, March 8, 1986; "Fear of purges and another Mariel," *Caribbean Report*, February 26, 1987; "Cuba endurece medidas ante corrupción oficial," *El Neuvo Herald*, November 26, 1988.

13. The list was compiled from information published in *El Neuvo Herald*, February 16, 1989.

14. U.S. Department of State, Bureau of Public Affairs, "Human Rights in Cuba: An Update" (Washington, D.C.: January 1989).

15. "The Current Human Rights Situation in Cuba As Viewed by the Committee for Human Rights," interview of committee members subsequently

edited, translated, and partially reprinted by the Cuban American National Foundation, *The Issue Is Cuba*, no. 2 (Washington, D.C.: 1988); for a broader discussion, see "Political Imprisonment in Cuba, A Special Report from Amnesty International," Cuban American National Foundation (1987). Also see "Americas Watch: Cuba viola los derechos humanos," *El Neuvo Herald*, January 29, 1989.

16. "Gorbachev Signs Treaty with Cuba," *New York Times*, April 5, 1989, p. 8A; "Gorbachev Attacks U.S. Regional Roles," *Washington Post*, April 5, 1989, p. 1; "Cuba and Russia," *The Economist*, April 8-14, 1989, pp. 47-48.

17. Consult Sergio Roca's "Cuba's International Economic Relations in the Late 1980s," pp. 101-121 and Jorge F. Perez-Lopez's "Cuban Hard-Currency Trade and Oil Reexports," pp. 123-155 in Roca, ed., *Socialist Cuba*.

18. "Gorbachev Attacks U.S. Regional Roles," *Washington Post*, April 5, 1989, p. 1.

19. The entire phrase is: "Those that dream that the Revolution could be defeated, are fooling themselves; they ignore that it is the continuation of our country's history, its highest phase, and it will live to be 40, to be 50, 60, and it will live to be 100 years old, and many more years, of that we have no doubt." President Castro's speech, January 1, 1989, *Granma Resumen Semanal*, January 15, 1989.

CHAPTER 4

The Impacts of "Restructuring" and "New Thinking" on Soviet-Vietnamese Relations

DANIEL S. PAPP

Since Mikhail Gorbachev became general secretary of the Communist Party of the Soviet Union in March 1985, he has unleashed an extensive wave of change and reform in the USSR that has extended across a broad range of social, political, economic, cultural, and foreign policy fields. Although it is far too soon to predict the end result of this wave of change and reform, it is clear that it has affected all aspects of Soviet life and policies.

This chapter examines only one parameter of the impact of Gorbachev's changes and reforms, namely, the effect they have had on Soviet relations with the Socialist Republic of Vietnam (SRV). It concentrates on two specific points: (1) the impact that "restructuring" has had on political and economic aspects of the Soviet-Vietnamese relationship, and (2) the impact that "new thinking" in Soviet foreign policy has had on Vietnam's foreign and defense policies. Before we turn to these issues, however, it will be useful to provide a brief overview of the evolution of Soviet-Vietnamese relations before Gorbachev became general secretary.[1]

SOVIET-VIETNAMESE RELATIONS BEFORE GORBACHEV

Soviet-Vietnamese relations passed through five distinct periods before 1985. The first period has no clear beginning, but may be presumed to start sometime in the 1920s when a number of Vietnamese, Ho Chi Minh included, began to receive training in the USSR. The first period ended in 1954 with the Geneva Agreements on Indochina.

For the most part, the pre-1954 period must be viewed as one of essential Soviet disengagement from Vietnam. Although it is well-documented that Vietnamese communists trained in the Soviet Union during this era, there are no reliable reports that the Soviet Union provided military or economic aid to Vietnamese communists before 1954. Indeed, even though Ho proclaimed Vietnamese independence in 1945, the USSR did not recognize Ho's government until 1950.

Soviet attitudes toward Vietnam began to change shortly after the 1954 Geneva Agreements were concluded. This marked the beginning of the second period of Soviet-Vietnamese relations, which lasted from 1954 to 1964. During this time, the Soviet Union jockeyed with China for presence and influence in Hanoi. Nevertheless, the Soviets refused to become too closely identified with or tied to Hanoi, probably because of Soviet concerns about how the United States might react to Ho's intentions to reunite the two Vietnamese "resettlement zones" created by the Geneva Accords.

The clearest indication that Soviet-Vietnamese relations had entered a second period came in 1955 when the two sides signed an economic and technical assistance agreement, and the Kremlin began to provide Hanoi with economic aid. Following Soviet President Voroshilov's 1957 trip to Hanoi, Soviet aid to Vietnam rose markedly, the result both of incipient Sino-Soviet rivalry and emerging Soviet activism in the Third World. Even so, Vietnam was not a high Soviet priority. The Kremlin had much more important interests elsewhere, and it continued to be concerned that Ho's support for the growing insurgency in South Vietnam might lead to confrontation with the United States.

There were also occasional indications of strain in Soviet-Vietnamese relations. For example, in 1963 the Vietnamese theoretical journal *Hoc Tap* declared that China would defend Vietnam in the event of a U.S. attack, but did not mention the USSR. Similarly, Vietnam refused to sign the nuclear test ban treaty despite Soviet pressure. By mid-1964, Nikita Khrushchev had become so disenchanted with events in Southeast Asia that he threatened to resign the Soviet Union's cochairmanship of the Geneva Control Commission on Indochina.

Shortly thereafter, Soviet-Vietnamese relations entered a third phase that began with the Americanization of the Vietnam conflict in 1964 and ended with the collapse of South Vietnam in 1975. At the beginning of this period, the USSR found itself in a dilemma. Having been accused by the Chinese of not being sufficiently aggressive in the fight against "U.S. imperialism," the Soviet Union undoubtedly felt pressured to respond to the U.S. attacks on North Vietnam that followed the August 1964 Gulf of Tonkin incidents. But the last thing the Soviets wanted was a confrontation with the United States over Vietnam.

Thus the Kremlin sought and found a middle ground, at least through late 1964 and early 1965. After barely reacting to the U.S. raids on North Vietnam following the Tonkin incidents, the new Soviet leaders (Leonid Brezhnev, Alexei Kosygin, and Nikolai Podgorny had ousted Nikita Khrushchev in October 1964) promised North Vietnam in November 1965 "the necessary assistance" to stave off U.S. "aggression." In February 1965 Kosygin even visited Hanoi, the first time a Soviet Politburo member had journeyed to North Vietnam since Voroshilov's 1957 visit. Clearly, Soviet-Vietnamese relations were warming.

However, embarrassingly for Kosygin and the Soviet Union, the United States launched bombing raids against North Vietnam during Kosygin's visit. Within a month, the U.S. was bombing North Vietnam on almost a daily basis. Gradually at first, and then more and more rapidly, Soviet aid levels to North Vietnam increased. For the next ten years, the USSR provided relatively large quantities of military and economic assistance to the Hanoi government. Although there were peaks and valleys in the Kremlin's aid levels to and political alignment with Vietnam between 1965 and 1975, the Soviet-Vietnamese relationship became much more intimate than it had been before.

Soviet-Vietnamese relations entered a fourth phase following North Vietnam's military victory over South Vietnam in 1975. Although the United States was by this time no longer a major player in Southeast Asian affairs, the Soviet Union maintained its previous regional activism both because of its rivalry with China and because of its own accentuated drive for global presence. Nevertheless, there was a discernible downturn in Soviet aid levels to Vietnam. For example, between 1975 and 1978 Soviet transfers of big-ticket military equipment to Hanoi virtually stopped. For its part, North Vietnam preferred to maintain close but not intimate ties with the Soviet Union. One measure of Vietnam's independence was Hanoi's refusal of Soviet requests to use Cam Ranh as a naval facility.

This brief period of transition ended in late 1978. During 1978, Vietnam began to expel its Chinese citizens, and in retaliation China ended economic assistance to Vietnam. In November 1978 the Soviet Union and Vietnam signed a Treaty of Friendship and Cooperation. The following month, Vietnam invaded Cambodia, and two months later, China invaded Vietnam. The Soviet Union immediately began an extensive airlift and sealift of military goods and supplies to Vietnam. The Soviet-Vietnamese alliance was sealed.

The final pre-Gorbachev period in Soviet-Vietnamese relations thus extended from 1979 to 1985. There are many measures of the intimacy of the relationship during this period. Le Duan, the general secretary of the Communist Party of Vietnam (CPV), visited the Soviet Union at least seven times between 1980 and 1985, and a steady flow of senior Soviet officials visited Hanoi, including Soviet Chief of Staff Nikolai Ogarkov (February 1982), Politburo members Mikhail Gorbachev (March 1982) and Geydar Aliyev (November 1983), and Secretariat member Vladimir Dolgikh (November 1984). Soviet economic assistance to Vietnam between 1981 and 1985 totaled somewhere between $3.2 and $5.2 billion, equal to all Soviet aid to Vietnam since the inception of the Kremlin's aid program to the country in 1955. Almost 100 percent of Vietnam's military equipment and supplies came from the USSR. After Vietnam granted the USSR port rights at Cam Ranh and airfield rights at Da Nang, the Soviets by early 1985 operated at least 30 naval units and 38 aircraft out of Vietnam.

Even so, hints occasionally surfaced that there were tensions in the Soviet-Vietnamese relationship. For example, when in late 1982 the USSR began moving slowly to improve its relations with China, concerns were raised in Hanoi about the level of Moscow's commitment to Vietnam. These concerns were further elevated when Vietnamese Defense Minister Van Tien Dung journeyed to Moscow twice in the aftermath of the April 1984 border fighting between Vietnam and China in an attempt to elicit more Soviet aid. He apparently received only verbal assurances of Moscow's support.[2] Similarly, during their trips to Vietnam, both Gorbachev and Aliyev obliquely noted Moscow's displeasure over Vietnam's mismanagement of Soviet economic aid. At the same time, Vietnam's continued military occupation of Cambodia complicated Soviet efforts to improve relations with noncommunist Southeast Asian states.

Despite these problems, Soviet-Vietnamese relations were intimate and cordial when Mikhail Gorbachev became CPSU general secretary in March 1985. Soviet-Vietnamese relations had transited several distinct phases that by 1985 had culminated in alliance.

TRANSITION: MARCH 1985 TO MID-1986

When Konstantin Chernenko died and Mikhail Gorbachev replaced him as CPSU general secretary, Vietnam sent a 16-man delegation headed by Prime Minister Pham Van Dong and Politburo member Truong Chinh to Moscow to attend the funeral. Chinh and Gorbachev held a private meeting that took place "in an atmosphere of fraternal friendship." The two men reportedly held "complete identity of views."[3]

Whatever the reality of Soviet-Vietnamese relations, Hanoi's greatest concern about Gorbachev undoubtedly was his continuing drive for improved relations with China, and the impact that that drive might have on the Kremlin's willingness to continue supporting Vietnam's presence in Cambodia. As previously mentioned, Sino-Soviet relations began to improve gradually as early as 1982, a trend that continued under Gorbachev. Shortly after Gorbachev assumed the general secretaryship, he met with Chinese First Vice-President Li Peng in Moscow, and in April 1985 Deng Xiaoping acted to improve Sino-Soviet relations by announcing that as far as China was concerned, the USSR could keep its military bases in Vietnam if the Vietnamese withdrew from Cambodia.[4] Throughout 1985 and early 1986, the pace of improvement in Sino-Soviet relations quickened as Soviet and Chinese officials continued to meet. The most important meeting took place in December 1985 when Deputy Foreign Minister Mikhail Kapitsa visited Beijing for ten days.

Hanoi was also concerned about the impact that improving U.S.-Soviet relations might have on Moscow's willingness to continue supporting Vietnam's Cambodian adventure. U.S. President Ronald Reagan had called on the Soviet Union publicly to help resolve regional conflicts including Cambodia,[5] and the resolution of regional conflicts was an agenda item at the November 1985 Reagan-Gorbachev Geneva summit meeting. Although neither Reagan's call nor the Geneva summit led to a U.S.-Soviet meeting of the minds on Cambodia or other regional conflicts, both undoubtedly raised Hanoi's level of concern.

On economic issues, Gorbachev through 1985 gave the Vietnamese no real cause for concern. Not yet having unveiled the breadth nor depth of his own plans to restructure the Soviet economy, Gorbachev gave no indication that he intended to force Vietnam to change its economic practices. To be sure, occasional Soviet spokespersons continued to express dissatisfaction with Vietnamese waste of Soviet aid, but even here the Soviets brought no real pressures for change to bear. In some respects, Vietnam even appeared to be ahead of the Soviet Union in coping with internal economic problems. For example, in February 1985, Vietnamese Politburo member Le Duc Tho described Vietnam's deplorable economic condition and discussed possible remedies, including agricultural development, material incentives, and even "capitalist economic reforms."[6] More significantly, the 8th Plenum of the 5th Vietnamese Communist Party Central Committee met in Hanoi in June 1985 and abolished subsidies for urban workers and cadres and ordered that they be paid in cash rather than kind. This new policy was viewed as a key step in the transition to an economic system based on merit and productivity rather than egalitarianism.[7] This clearly indicated an intention on the part of the CPV to move away from ideology and toward pragmatism in its economic practices. But as is so often the case, intentions proved difficult to implement. In November 1985 the CPV paper *Nhan Dan* admitted that the reforms "could take years" to put into place, and that a serious gap existed between "the political line and practical action."[8] Some Western observers even argued that Vietnam's efforts to introduce economic reform rapidly led to a further deterioration of the Vietnamese economy.[9]

By mid-1986, then, with the exception of the growth of Vietnamese concern stemming from ever-more-cordial Sino-Soviet relations, little had changed in Soviet-Vietnamese relations as the result of Gorbachev or his reforms. This was to be expected for several distinct reasons. First, Gorbachev's reforms were only just beginning to get under way in the USSR. The new Soviet leader had spent most of his first year in power putting his own domestic political house in order, and did not truly detail his broader intentions for restructuring until the February 1986 27th Party Congress. Second, the Vietnamese leadership was well-entrenched. Four of the "Inner Circle of Five" CPV Politburo members—Le Duan, Truong Chinh, Pham Van Dong, and Le Duc Tho—had been at or near the pinnacle of power in Vietnam for decades. Despite their country's extensive reliance on the USSR for economic and military assistance, it is doubtful if Gorbachev could have swayed them from their chosen path even had he attempted it. And third, in some respects Vietnam was actually ahead of the USSR in coming to grips with its economic problems. Most of Vietnam's senior leadership recognized the reality of their country's dire economic straits and accepted the need for radical reform and change. Their problem was their inability to implement reform and change successfully.

RESTRUCTURING, ECONOMIC POLICY, AND SOVIET-VIETNAMESE RELATIONS SINCE MID-1986

The constancy that prevailed in Soviet-Vietnamese relations during the first 15 months of Gorbachev's tenure ended during the second half of 1986, at least in part because of two significant changes in the CPV leadership. The first major change took place in July 1986, when long-time party leader Le Duan died.[10] Truong Chinh, who was named general secretary to replace him, journeyed to Moscow shortly after becoming general secretary and met with Gorbachev. According to all reports, the meeting was amiable, although it was notable that Truong Chinh in one public comment mentioned the need to use Soviet aid more effectively.

The second set of changes occurred in December 1986 at the 6th CPV Congress. Truong Chinh lost both his Politburo seat and the general secretaryship, and Prime Minister Pham Van Dong and senior Politburo member Le Duc Tho were removed from the Politburo as well. Nguyen Van Linh, generally viewed as a reformer, was named the new CPV general secretary.

Although it is impossible to discern the intraparty machinations that led to this second set of senior personnel changes, it was clear from Truong Chinh's Political Report to the CPV Congress that Vietnam's dire economic straits played a major role in the changes. No one could deny that Vietnam's economy was a disaster, and that past policies and recent reforms had not worked. Although few specific programs were put into place, delegates to the 6th CPV Congress unanimously agreed that "renovation" (*canh tan*) was necessary throughout the economy.

The extent to which the Soviet Union pressured or influenced Vietnamese leaders to move toward renovation is not evident. To a considerable extent, the concept of "renovation" may have had roots in Vietnam, not the Soviet Union. As noted above, the Vietnamese economy was a disaster that could not be ignored, and the CPV had begun its own reform efforts even before Gorbachev launched his restructuring. Granted, Vietnam's reform efforts had not worked, but they were nevertheless in place. At the same time, with new leaders emerging in Vietnam, it was reasonable to expect them to begin to implement policies different from the failed policies of their predecessors.

On the other hand, it is also reasonable to assume that the Soviet Union insisted on changed economic policies within Vietnam, both because the USSR provided such large quantities of aid to Vietnam at a time when the USSR itself required large amounts of investment capital, and because Vietnam was wasting large quantities of Soviet aid. Indeed, with restructuring beginning to take hold in the USSR in late 1986, Gorbachev and other Soviet leaders could scarcely have legitimized sending billions of rubles to Vietnam to be used in ways that would not have been acceptable in the Soviet economy. With both Vietnamese and Soviets acknowledging publicly that Vietnam had wasted large quantities of Soviet aid,[11] continued Soviet provision of large quantities of economic aid in the absence of changed Vietnamese management practices simply could not have been acceptable to the Kremlin.

As if to drive this home to the Vietnamese, the Kremlin sent Igor Ligachev, the number-two man in the Soviet Politburo at the time, to Hanoi to attend the 6th Party Congress in December 1986. Ligachev carried both a carrot and a stick to Vietnam. Ligachev's carrot was the promise that Soviet aid would be twice as great between 1986 and 1990 as compared to the previous five years—that is, roughly equivalent to the grand total of Soviet aid to Vietnam between 1954 and 1986. (Western sources placed the 1986–90 aid promise at between $11.7 and $13.2 billion.)[12] On the other hand, Ligachev's stick was his regularly repeated warning that the Vietnamese must better utilize Soviet aid.[13] To make sure that Hanoi did not miss the point, the Central Committee of the CPSU held a special one-day conference in Moscow in early January 1987 to discuss the need for "improvement" in Soviet-Vietnamese economic cooperation. The conference observed that "more than a little success" had been attained in the Soviet Union's aid program to Vietnam, but stressed that "the most serious attention" had to be devoted to "creative rethinking" and "improvement of work of enterprises built or being built in Vietnam by the Soviet Union."[14] It is also probable that the Soviets stressed the necessity for better Vietnamese utilization of Soviet aid during the week-long mid-January session of the twelfth meeting of the Soviet-Vietnamese Intergovernmental Commission on Economic, Scientific, and Technical Cooperation.[15]

Clearly, the Soviets were not pleased with the Vietnamese use of aid. The Soviets may well have chosen to emphasize this long-simmering issue at this time because they believed they could better pressure the new Vietnamese leadership into making changes. Additionally, with their promise of more economic aid, the Soviets could bring more leverage to bear. Nevertheless, it must be reiterated that the Soviets pushed the Vietnamese in the direction the Vietnamese already were heading, that is, toward economic reform.

Even though economic issues took a backseat to foreign policy issues during Soviet Foreign Minister Eduard Shevardnadze's three-day stop in Vietnam during his March 1987 six-nation Southeast Asia trip, economic issues were not completely ignored. The joint statement issued at the end of Shevardnadze's visit noted complete Soviet and Vietnamese agreement on the two countries' respective evaluations of the status of Soviet-Vietnamese economic relations and on the necessity to develop and implement more effective forms of Soviet-Vietnamese cooperation.[16]

The seriousness with which the Vietnamese—and the Soviets— viewed Vietnam's waste of Soviet aid returned to center stage on two separate occasions during May. In early May, the CPV Politburo met to examine ways to improve the efficiency of use of Soviet aid, stressing that the changes that they intended to put into place to achieve this end were in "full accord with the spirit and goals of the restructuring under way in the Soviet Union." Soviet commentary on the CPV Politburo meeting noted that Vietnam's past policies had "often led to the irrational utilization of the extensive Soviet aid."[17]

Later in May, CPV leader Nguyen Van Linh traveled to the USSR for four days of meetings with Gorbachev and other Soviet leaders. Linh and Gorbachev held talks on several occasions, and covered both foreign policy and economic issues. Gorbachev and Linh "exchanged viewpoints" on both issue areas, and Gorbachev noted that the two countries were at "different levels of development."[18] Soviet domestic media coverage of the discussions stated that the two leaders held "a discussion on questions of Soviet-Vietnamese economic cooperation" that took place "in an atmosphere of frankness, mutual understanding, and cordiality"—in other words, disagreements arose.[19] In his speech at the state dinner held for Linh at the Kremlin, Gorbachev emphasized that a socialist state had "only one effective way" to expedite progress, "by decisively abandoning outdated work methods, bringing popular initiative and enterprise into play fully, and bringing out the potentialities of socialism." Continuing, Gorbachev complained that "the weaker aspects" of Soviet-Vietnamese "economic bonds and their failure to correspond with the new situation have begun to show."[20]

Clearly, Gorbachev and Linh had had some disagreements over economic policy, even though it was not possible to discern what the specific issues of disagreement were. Two possible areas of disagreement were over how reforms in Vietnam and in Soviet-Vietnamese economic relations should be implemented. A third possible area of disagreement was the extent to which the USSR shared in the blame for the problems. Indeed, a month after Linh's visit, a special conference called by the CPSU Central Committee observed that "much good" had come from Soviet aid to Vietnam, Mongolia, and Cuba, but "serious shortcomings" existed in "the activity of a number" of Soviet ministries and departments.[21]

Whatever the cause or extent of Soviet-Vietnamese disagreements, Linh during his May visit nevertheless gave the Soviets, or more specifically the 27th CPSU Congress, credit for "inspiring" the economic reforms that the CPV was attempting to implement. Linh further identified three "major economic programs" that his country was trying to operationalize: increased food production, greater consumer goods output, and more production for export.[22] For their part, the Soviets applauded the general thrust of Vietnam's efforts in this direction.

By mid-1987, then, a much clearer picture had emerged about the impact of Soviet restructuring on Vietnamese economic reforms and Soviet-Vietnamese economic relations. Despite having announced and even implemented some of their reforms in 1985 before the Soviets had announced or implemented theirs, Vietnam's reforms had not fared well. This fact, plus the combination of a new leadership in Hanoi and Soviet willingness to extend greater quantities of economic aid to Vietnam if the Vietnamese modified and accelerated their reform policies, allowed the Soviets to influence, but not control, the pace and direction of new economic reform in Vietnam. Soviet-Vietnamese disagreements on undefined economic issues eventuated, but these disagreements were never serious enough to disrupt the continuing cordiality in the relationship. Soviet economic assistance to Vietnam continued to buttress the Vietnamese economy, with the Kremlin having completed 250 "economic enterprises" in Vietnam by the end of 1987.[23]

By the beginning of 1989, then, the Soviets remained concerned about inefficient Vietnamese use of Soviet economic aid and continued to push the Vietnamese for improvement. But the Soviets were not concerned enough about Vietnamese inefficiency to reduce aid.[24] At the same time, it was evident that the Soviets and Vietnamese had somewhat different views of the state of their relationship. Indeed, while the Soviets preferred to see themselves as the senior partner in the relationship, and obviously held the preponderance of coercive influence in the relationship as a result of their extensive economic and military assistance to Hanoi, Vietnam's leadership saw things differently. To the CPV leaders, Vietnam intended to set its own economic course, perhaps in cooperation with the Soviet Union, but never in subservience. This sense of being equal partners in reform was most evident in Linh's November 1988 comments on the tenth anniversary of the Soviet-Vietnamese Treaty of Friendship and Cooperation:

The policy of [Soviet] restructuring and the policy of [Vietnamese] renewal have opened up new possibilities for efficient, mutually advantageous, and mutually responsible cooperation.... Vietnam and the Soviet Union are fully resolved to switch the old mechanism of Vietnamese-Soviet economic relations from the rails of bureaucratic centralization and undemocratic administration onto the path of the elaboration and introduction of new progressive forms of the international socialist division of labor, the development of productive collaboration, economic integration, and the expansion of direct ties between sectors and productive enterprises.[25]

In sum, then, the impact of Soviet restructuring on Vietnamese reform and Soviet-Vietnamese economic relations may be simply stated: Soviet restructuring clearly influenced some of the trends in Vietnamese renewal, but it was neither the initiator nor the determinator of Vietnam's economic reform effort.

NEW THINKING, FOREIGN POLICY, AND
SOVIET-VIETNAMESE RELATIONS SINCE MID-1986

As we have seen, Vietnam's own economic situation had become so dire by the mid-1980s that it was apparent to almost everyone that change and reform had to be instituted in Vietnam's economic practices. Because of this awareness, the USSR's own economic restructuring efforts caused little concern in Hanoi even though the USSR and Vietnam sometimes disagreed over the specifics of reforms and how they might affect Soviet-Vietnamese relations.

The same was not true of changes in the USSR's foreign policy, described as "new thinking" by Mikhail Gorbachev. Three specific aspects of Gorbachev's new thinking directly affected Soviet-Vietnamese relations and raised sizable concerns in Hanoi about the future course of Soviet policy. These three aspects were Gorbachev's accelerated drive to improve relations with China, the implications of new thinking for Soviet military presence in Southeast Asia, and the question of whether the USSR would continue to support Vietnam's military occupation of Cambodia.

Gorbachev's accelerated drive to improve Sino-Soviet relations evoked especially great concern in Hanoi. Gorbachev frequently emphasized that under new thinking, the Soviet Union would pursue friendly relations with China. For example, in his July 1986 Vladivostok speech, Gorbachev praised the "noticeable improvement in relations" that had taken place between Moscow and Beijing, and called for even closer Sino-Soviet relations in the future.[26]

In one sense, this should not have further perturbed the Vietnamese. As previously noted, Sino-Soviet relations had begun to improve as early as 1982 when Leonid Brezhnev was still in power, and this trend continued under both Yuri Andropov and Konstantin Chernenko, Gorbachev's new thinking, at least as it applied to China, was therefore simply a continuation of already-in-place Soviet policy.

In another sense, however, new thinking introduced new elements to the Sino-Soviet rapprochement. It was these new elements that further heightened Vietnam's already existing concern. At least in part because of the impetus provided by Gorbachev's new thinking, the Soviets and the Chinese solved their border dispute along the Amur River, began building a cross-border railway, and signed a series of new trade agreements. Additionally, the entire political climate of Sino-Soviet relations improved noticeably. Indeed, by the time Chinese and Soviet representatives met in Beijing for the eleventh round of political consultations in October 1987, the Cambodian question was the only apparent major area of disagreement. When in subsequent meetings the Soviets and Chinese narrowed their disagreement over Cambodia,[27] Vietnam's concern that its interests would be jettisoned by the Soviets in favor of improved Moscow-Beijing relations escalated even more. Gorbachev's decision to visit China in May 1989 added to Vietnam's fears, despite Soviet assurances that Moscow-Hanoi relations would not be threatened by the Sino-Soviet summit.

New thinking also implied that the Soviet Union should rely less on military parameters of power in its efforts to achieve foreign policy objectives. This clearly had implications for the Soviet Union's military presence at Cam Ranh and Da Nang. In the pre-Gorbachev era, Vietnam recognized that the USSR's desire to detain port and airfield rights at Cam Ranh and Da Nang gave it a certain degree of leverage over the USSR. From Vietnam's perspective, if the Soviets ever moved too far or too fast in their accommodation with Beijing at the expense of Hanoi, Hanoi could simply reduce or eliminate those Soviet port and airfield rights. This was a powerful lever given the Kremlin's evident desire to maintain and maximize access to both sites.

As early as July 1986, Gorbachev in his Vladivostok speech implied that he would be willing to end the USSR's military presence in Vietnam if the United States ended its military presence in the Philippines. This undoubtedly caused Vietnam's leaders to wonder if they retained as much leverage as they previously believed they had had. When Gorbachev made an explicit base-trade offer in his September 1989 Krasnoyarsk speech,[28] Hanoi's concerns about its limited leverage over the USSR probably escalated even more.[29]

Of course, there undoubtedly were motivations to Gorbachev's base-trade offer in addition to new thinking. The Soviet leader could have been seeking to complicate U.S. negotiations with the Philippines on extending the base agreement, or he could have been seeking to gain a propaganda advantage over the United States in Southeast Asia by portraying the United States as the country whose refusal to eliminate its regional military bases prolonged the superpower rivalry in Southeast Asia. From Hanoi's perspective, however, the Soviets may well have had a more sinister purpose: to gain for the USSR leverage over Vietnam by communicating to the Vietnamese that the

Kremlin was no longer as wedded to its bases as it once was, and that under certain conditions it might abandon its bases. For Vietnam's leaders, then, new thinking, by causing the Kremlin to question its reliance on the military component of foreign policy, had potentially lessened the amount of leverage that Hanoi held over Moscow as a result of port and airfield access rights Hanoi granted the USSR.

As serious as both the Sino-Soviet and access rights issues were, the impact of new thinking on the Kremlin's willingness to continue supporting Hanoi's military occupation of Cambodia was probably even more foreboding as seen from Hanoi. Even though the USSR had supported Vietnam's policy positions on Cambodia ever since Vietnam invaded Cambodia in 1978, it had become increasingly clear during the second half of the 1980s that the Kremlin preferred that Vietnam withdraw from Cambodia.

There were several reasons for this. First, Vietnam's occupation of Cambodia—or more specifically, Soviet support for Vietnam's occupation of Cambodia—complicated the Kremlin's efforts to improve relations with China. Second, it also frustrated Soviet efforts to better relations with other Southeast Asian states. Similarly, Soviet support for Vietnam's presence in Cambodia even affected adversely Soviet-U.S. relations, Soviet-European relations, and Soviet relations with much of the Third World. With new thinking insisting that political solutions were preferable to military solutions in resolving regional conflicts, and with so many Soviet foreign policy objectives being complicated by Vietnam's occupation of Cambodia, it was understandable that the Kremlin wanted Vietnam to withdraw and that Hanoi might have been concerned that the Kremlin might end its support for Vietnam's military adventure in Cambodia.

Perhaps surprisingly, however, the Soviet Union manifested no overt pressure on Vietnam to leave Cambodia. Instead, Moscow preferred to maintain a public posture of solidarity with Vietnam on most issues related to Vietnam through mid-1986. Thus the Soviets supported not only the Vietnamese occupation of Cambodia, but also Vietnam's stated intention to withdraw from Cambodia by 1990 and Vietnam's preference for a postwithdrawal political settlement. Occasionally, the Soviets also insisted that a solution to the Cambodian problem depended on "normalization of Sino-Vietnamese relations."[30]

In late 1986, the Soviets began to assume a more active posture on Cambodia. At the ninth session of Sino-Soviet political consultatations, held in Beijing, October 6–14, 1986, the Soviets for the first time discussed Cambodia with the Chinese. Although the two sides made little progress, the fact that the two sides even discussed Cambodia was a significant step. Six months later, in April 1987, the USSR and China again examined Cambodian issues at the tenth session of Sino-Soviet political consultations.[31] Clearly, the Soviets had adopted a more active posture on Cambodia.

Evidence also began to mount in early 1987 that Vietnam and the Soviet Union did not see eye-to-eye on how the Cambodian conflict should end. This disagreement became most apparent during CPV General Secretary Nguyen Van Linh's May 1987 trip to the Soviet Union. While in Moscow, Linh, during a dinner speech, insisted that a political settlement in Cambodia exclude the "Pol Pot clique" from the Khmer Rouge, but Gorbachev in his own dinner speech pointedly failed to mention such a condition.[32] Even more telling, the final communiqué for the meeting observed that "an in-depth exchange of views" had taken place "in an atmosphere of traditional friendship and mutual understanding." The final communiqué also offered the curious formula that national reconciliation in Cambodia had to be achieved through "political means" with "the involvement in this or that form of all sides concerned."[33] Obviously, the Soviet-Vietnamese disagreement was serious.

Meanwhile, the Soviet Union quietly pursued a series of diplomatic contacts with Thailand, Indonesia, and Malaysia in an effort to impart new momentum to relations between the Soviets and the Association of Southeast Asian Nations (ASEAN) and the Cambodian negotiating process. More proof of the Kremlin's desire to resolve the Cambodian conflict is evident in the Soviet efforts to arrange a meeting between Cambodian Premier Hun Sen and resistance leader Prince Norodom Sihanouk.[34] Eventually, the two Cambodians met in Paris in early December 1987. They agreed that a political solution to the war had to be found involving all parties and guaranteed by an international conference.

The Soviets also tried to influence the Cambodian government to meet with Khieu Samphan, the Khmer Rouge leader, but this time they were not successful.[35] The emerging peace process was further complicated in January, following the second Sihanouk-Hun Sen meeting when Sihanouk refused to continue discussions unless he also met with Vietnamese officials. The Vietnamese refused. For all practical purposes, the process had become deadlocked. What is important here for our purposes, however, is the fact that the Vietnamese had blocked an initiative launched by the Soviets. Thus it was evident that Vietnam and the USSR disagreed over the urgency of ending the conflict, the way in which the conflict should be ended, or both.

Nevertheless, despite Vietnam's unwillingness to meet with Sihanouk, the Soviets continued to try to find the key to a political settlement. Soviet and U.S. officials met on a number of occasions in the first half of 1988 to discuss Cambodia, and in March Soviet Deputy Foreign Minister Igor Rogachev met with Indochinese deputy foreign ministers in Phnom Penh. At the meeting, the deputy foreign ministers agreed to speed up efforts to achieve national reconciliation. Following his Phnom Penh visit, Rogachev traveled to the Philippines, Malaysia, Thailand, and Indonesia. Cambodia figured prominently in discussions in all four countries; but the real key to a Cambodian settlement remained Vietnam. Through March, Hanoi had changed its positions little, despite continued Soviet prodding.[36]

This soon changed. In April, Nguyen Van Linh visited Moscow and told the Soviets that Vietnam's withdrawal from Cambodia would be accelerated, and that Hanoi would strengthen its efforts to improve relations with China. The following month, the Vietnamese announced they would withdraw 50,000 troops from Cambodia by the end of 1988 and reaffirmed their intention to complete the withdrawal by 1990. Additionally, Hanoi confirmed that a Vietnamese delegation would attend the resurrected "cocktail party" negotiattions, now known as the Jakarta Informal Meeting, scheduled to be held in Bogor, Indonesia, in late July 1988. The Soviets profusely praised these Vietnamese positions.

For their part, the Vietnamese undoubtedly remained concerned about the implications of the steady improvement in Sino-Soviet relations for Soviet-Vietnamese relations. Indeed, even though the Kremlin verbally supported Vietnam in March 1988 when the Chinese-Vietnamese dispute over the Spratly Islands escalated once again,[37] the Soviet position had no visible impact on Sino-Soviet relations.

On the eve of the Bogor talks, CPV General Secretary Nguyen Van Linh visited the USSR, ostensibly for a vacation. During his stay in Moscow he met with Gorbachev, and the two men agreed that their countries were "prepared actively to facilitate the defusing of the situation" in Cambodia. They also noted that China could make a "weighty contribution" to the resolution of the Cambodian problem, and expressed high hopes for the Bogor talks.[38]

Despite Linh's and Gorbachev's optimism, the talks produced little other than an agreement to meet again. Nevertheless, that the talks had taken place was significant in itself. The Soviet Union made known its position on the Bogor discussions in an August 3 Ministry of Foreign Affairs statement praising the participants and affirming its own "readiness to contribute ... to the development of the process of settlement" in Cambodia.[39]

Throughout the rest of 1988, the Soviets continued to stress the need for a political settlement, national reconciliation, and their own willingness to help the peace process along. Soviet Deputy Foreign Minister Rogachev, for example, stressed all these points during his November 1988 trip to Hanoi.

Meanwhile, Vietnam had been seeking to initiate a dialogue with China on Cambodia. In November, Vietnam's Foreign Minister Thach told reporters at a Hanoi press conference that Vietnam had offered to hold talks with China on Cambodia, but China had refused. The following month Thach told the 8th Vietnamese National Assembly that Vietnam was prepared for "direct dialogue" with China on bilateral issues.[40] Clearly, Vietnam had felt pressure emanating from Moscow.

The Soviets soon turned up the pressure even more. In early February Soviet Foreign Minister Shevardnadze traveled to Beijing and reached a nine-point agreement on Cambodia with China. Among other points, the Chinese and the Soviets agreed on the need for a political solution to the conflict, "an effective control mechanism" to supervise Vietnam's withdrawal, an end to foreign military aid, the maintenance of peace in Cambodia, and free elections.[41]

By early 1989 it was clear that the Soviets were intent on a Vietnamese withdrawal from Cambodia. At the same time, they were equally intent on solidifying their emerging relationship with Beijing. New thinking played a significant role in both of these intentions.

The impact of new thinking should not be overstated, however. Moscow's thinking was not sufficiently new to influence it to jettison its support for Vietnam's occupation of Cambodia, but only to apply pressure through a variety of means to influence Cambodia to adhere to and possibly accelerate its previously stated withdrawal date. Thus, in the final analysis Moscow, even with its new thinking, was unwilling—or unable—to force Hanoi to withdraw from Cambodia before it was prepared to withdraw.

CONCLUSION

Restructuring and new thinking clearly have had an impact on Soviet-Vietnamese relations, but that impact is not as sizable as may be imagined at first blush. It is evident that Soviet demands that Vietnam employ Soviet aid more effectively have influenced the Vietnamese to alter some of their domestic economic policies, but at the same time it is clear that the Vietnamese were changing their domestic economic policies even before the Soviets made their demands. Similarly, the combination of Soviet desires for better relations with China and a political solution to the Cambodian conflict both increased pressures on Vietnam to withdraw from Cambodia, but one must be careful not to attribute too much to new thinking. Even before new thinking became the foreign policy vogue in Moscow, the Soviets sought to better their relations with Beijing, and Vietnam had committed itself to a military withdrawal from Cambodia by 1990 as early as August 1985.[42]

Having cautioned that one must be careful not to attribute too much influence to restructuring and new thinking, one must be equally careful not to dismiss the influence they have had. Both have significantly reduced the freedom that Vietnam may have had to maneuver away from previously stated positions. Given the combination of Vietnam's insistence that it will reform its domestic economic practices, extensive Vietnamese reliance on Soviet economic assistance, and the Kremlin's clear desire as implied in restructuring that Vietnam carry out its economic reforms, it is virtually unthinkable that Vietnam could now renege or roll back its own reforms. Similarly, with Hanoi's own declarations that it will withdraw its military forces from Cambodia by 1990 and the USSR's obvious desire for a political settlement to the conflict, it is virtually unthinkable that Hanoi would renege on its withdrawal commitment. There is no doubt that the added impetus that new thinking provided to improved Sino-Soviet relations added to Hanoi's uncertainty about its own status in Moscow. Likewise, new thinking's emphasis on nonmilitary dimensions of foreign policy raised questions in Hanoi about the degree of importance Moscow attached to its military bases at Cam Ranh and Da Nang.

All told, restructuring and new thinking have contributed to change both in Vietnam and in Soviet-Vietnamese relations. But, at most, a balanced assessment forces the conclusion that restructuring and new thinking influenced Vietnam to move more rapidly in directions toward which it was already headed.

NOTES

1. For another view of the evolution of Soviet-Vietnamese relations, see Douglas Pike, *Vietnam and the Soviet Union: Anatomy of an Alliance* (Boulder, CO: Westview Press, 1987).

2. Paul Quinn-Judge, "Return to Moscow," *Far Eastern Economic Review*, August 2, 1984, pp. 24-26.

3. Radio Moscow, March 14, 1985, as reported in *Daily Report-Soviet Union* (Foreign Broadcast Information Service, hereafter FBIS), March 14, 1985, p. E1.

4. Deng also stated that the Vietnamese occupation of Cambodia was the easiest of the three major obstacles to overcome in Sino-Soviet relations. (The other obstacles were the Soviet military occupation of Afghanistan and the Soviet military buildup on the Sino-Soviet border.) For Deng's statement, see Richard Nations, "Great Leap Sideways," *Far Eastern Economic Review*, May 30, 1985, pp. 15-16.

5. See Ronald Reagan's October 24, 1985 speech to the United Nations, in the the *New York Times*, October 25, 1985.

6. *L'Humanité* (Paris), February 15, 1985.

7. William J. Duiker, "Vietnam in 1985: Searching for Solutions," *Asian Survey* 26 (January 1986): 109.

8. *Nhan Dan*, November 13-15, 1985, as reported in *Indochina Chronology* 4, no. 4 (October-December, 1985): 6. For additional commentary on Vietnam's economic problems and reforms, see Nayan Chanda, "The New Revolution," *Far Eastern Economic Review*, April 10, 1986, pp. 24-28.

9. Charles McGregor, "The Sino-Vietnamese Relationship and the Soviet Union," *Adelphi Papers*, no. 232 (Autumn 1988): 73. See also John H. Esterline, "Vietnam in 1986: An Uncertain Tiger," *Asian Survey* 27 (January 1987): 92-96.

10. The Soviet delegation to Le Duan's funeral included Politburo member and Council of Ministers Chairman N. I. Ryzhkov, Head of the CPSU International Department A. F. Dobrynin, and Deputy Foreign Minister (and former Soviet Ambassador to Vietnam) B. N. Chaplin.

11. The November 3, 1986 issue of *Nhan Dan* admitted that Vietnam had wasted "billions of rubles of Soviet aid in recent years." See *Indochina Chronology* 5, no. 4 (October-December 1986): 5. Thai sources reported that the USSR

had sent $7.5 billion in military aid alone to Vietnam between 1982 and 1986. See *The Nation* (Bangkok), May 15, 1987.

12. Reuters Press Release, December 15, 1986.

13. *Pravda*, December 19, 1986; and *Izvestiya*, December 19, 1986.

14. Radio Moscow, January 5, 1987, as reported in *Daily Report-Soviet Union* (FBIS) January 6, 1987, p. E1. See also Gerald Segal, "The USSR and Asia in 1987: Signs of a Major Effort," *Asian Survey* 28, no. 1 (Janaury 1988): 3.

15. *Pravda*, January 19, 1987.

16. For a text of the joint statement, see *Pravda*, March 14, 1987.

17. *Izvestiya*, May 11, 1987.

18. *Pravda*, May 19, 1987.

19. Radio Moscow, May 19, 1987, as reported in *Daily Report-Soviet Union* (FBIS) May 21, 1987, pp. E3-4.

20. *Pravda*, May 20, 1987.

21. *Pravda*, June 23, 1987.

22. *Pravda*, May 20, 1987.

23. Radio Moscow, January 14, 1988, as reported in *Daily Report-Soviet Union* (FBIS) January 19, 1988, p. 36.

24. See Sophie Quinn-Judge and Murray Hiebert, "Ten Year Itch: Soviets Admit Much of Economic Aid to Hanoi Was Wasted," *Far Eastern Economic Review*, November 10, 1988, p. 23.

25. *Pravda*, November 2, 1988.

26. For the complete text of Gorbachev's Vladivostok speech, see Moscow Television Service, July 28, 1986, as reported in *Daily Report-Soviet Union* (FBIS) July 29, 1986, pp. R1-20.

27. By early February 1989, the USSR and China had reduced their disagreements over Cambodia to the point where they could issue a joint nine-point agreement on Cambodia at the conclusion of Soviet Foreign Minister Shevardnadze's three-day trip to Beijing. This will be discussed in more detail later.

28. For the complete text of Gorbachev's Krasnoyarsk speech, see *Pravda*, September 18, 1988.

29. See Murray Hiebert, "Carping About Cam Ranh: Hanoi Is Unhappy Over Moscow's Offer on the Base," *Far Eastern Economic Review*, October 27, 1988, p. 27.

30. For example, see Gorbachev's Vladivostok speech, as broadcast by Moscow Television Service, July 28, 1986, as reported in *Daily Report-Soviet Union* (FBIS) July 29, 1986, p. R17.

31. See *Bangkok Post*, April 22, 1987.

32. *Pravda*, May 20, 1987.

33. *Pravda*, May 22, 1987.

34. *Washington Post*, May 6, 1988. See also Robert Delfs, "The Sihanouk Card," *Far Eastern Economic Review*, February 11, 1988, p. 35.

35. Nayan Chanda, "Marriage Made in Moscow," *Far Eastern Economic Review*, June 9, 1988, p. 17.

36. See "Moscow's Cambodia Push," *Asiaweek*, May 13, 1988, p. 36.

37. For an example of the Soviet position, see Radio Moscow, April 6, 1988, as reported in *Daily Report-Soviet Union* (FBIS) April 7, 1988, p. 8.

38. TASS, July 20, 1988, as reported in *Daily Report-Soviet Union* (FBIS) August 8, 1988, p. 16.

39. TASS, August 3, 1988, as reported in *Daily Report-Soviet Union* (FBIS) August 3, 1988, p. 15.

40. Nayan Chanda, "Taking the Soft Line: Vietnam Signals China It Wants Improved Relations," *Far Eastern Economic Review*, December 8, 1988, p. 27-28.

41. For the text of the joint statement, see *Pravda*, February 6, 1989. See also Nayan Chanda, "The Sticking Points," *Far Eastern Economic Review*, February 16, 1989, p. 11.

42. This commitment was contained in the communiqué issued at the end of the August 1985 Indochinese Foreign Ministers Conference. See *Vietnam Courier*, September 1985, p. 2.

CHAPTER 5

Glasnost and Afghanistan: The Mirage in the Desert

STEPHEN BLANK

To what degree have the domestic policies of the government of Afghanistan since 1985 followed or been influenced by the Gorbachev regime's program known as glasnost or perestroika? Obviously qualitative differences exist between Soviet and Afghan society and hence between Gorbachev's program and Afghan policies. Another reason for the difference is the continuing civil war between the Kabul regime and the Mujaheddin. However, an answer to the question also depends to a great degree on Moscow's ability to influence the internal policies of the Democratic Republic of Afghanistan (DRA). Ascertaining the degree and effectiveness of such influence is decidedly problematical.[1]

Earlier accounts of the Afghan regime from the revolution in April 1978 until 1985 when Gorbachev took power in Moscow generally traced a picture of ever greater and deeper Soviet intervention into the Afghan government's daily routine. Ministries were supposedly dominated by Soviet advisors, and Babrak Karmal's security and policies were similarly organized. Sovietization was in full swing and recurring documentation of economic integration, exploitation, educational Sovietization, and even plans for the Balkanization of Afghanistan's territories and peoples along Soviet nationality policy guidelines were accurately reported.[2] Yet during 1978-79 the People's Democratic Party of Afghanistan (PDPA) regime pursued policies of radical socialism in land reform, educational secularization, antireligious campaigns, emancipation of women, and so on, that reportedly contradicted what Soviet advisors were recommending (according to Western sources) and that clearly undermined the PDPA's domestic support. Indeed, such policies triggered the revolution against the PDPA that ultimately forced Moscow to intervene.[3]

If so, what was Moscow's real influence and its real advice concerning construction of a socialist Afghanistan at that time? Moreover, after the invasion of 1979 Babrak Karmal radically shifted regime policies toward more moderate objectives of accommodation with Islam, less rapid reform, and repeated if largely insincere efforts to effect some sort of national unity or fatherland front-type regime with the rebels. Such a regime would be reminiscent of similar arrangements in Eastern Europe 40 years ago.[4] Supposedly these policies, all of which had failed to win support before 1986, were also Moscow-dictated ones. Since Najibullah's rise to power in 1985-86 he too has evidently, under Soviet pressure, followed policies along notably similar lines under the rubric of "national reconciliation," a policy also advocated by him and Moscow for Kampuchea (Cambodia), another war-torn country. As of today he has also failed to win support and is visibly subject to intense Soviet pressure to conform to Moscow's dictates. At the same time the recent appointment of Deputy Foreign Minister Vorontsov as ambassador to Kabul, while he operates out of Moscow and retains his full ministerial status, testifies to Moscow's intention to control the future of Afghanistan. So do the economic and educational policies discussed below.

The process by which Moscow was drawn into a massive military intervention indicates that during 1978-79 it came to realize or believe that only direct and massive control of the government allowed for "proper" policy formation and execution to end the civil war. Yet this control has not been enough and the entire process until now bears striking similarity to the U.S. quandary in Vietnam from 1954 to 1975. Even when the superpower patron takes over the regime and the brunt of fighting it does not seem to be able to translate its power into effective and lasting influence (i.e., making and implementing its policy preferences). The gradual attentuation of Soviet capacity to dominate developments within communist parties abroad (France, Italy, Vietnam, China, North Korea) and even in some Eastern bloc societies (Poland, Hungary, and Rumania to considerable degrees) certainly has also contributed to this process vis-à-vis Afghanistan. For example, it appears that Afghanistan's government has considerably slowed Moscow's movement to a negotiated settlement, such as that of Geneva in 1988, fearing abandonment by its patron and the reconstitution of a less communist, or less visibly so, regime.⁵ To reach this agreement Moscow has had to expend considerable political and economic capital to win Kabul's assent to the treaty, and Vorontsov's appointment may also signify Kabul's continuing resistance to the treaty's implementation. Therefore, it seems that Kabul's real attitude is publicly constrained to conceal its dependence on Soviet military, economic, and diplomatic support.

Indeed, Moscow has been forced to take greater control of the Afghan economy and education process as the regime's incapacity and unwillingness to reform became more manifest. In this connection the widely reported fact of the Afghan equivalent of the KGB, the WAD (formerly KHAD), being the most efficient and effective arm of the regime, points to the heavy investment by Moscow and East Berlin in training it and in creating the necessary infrastructure for Sovietization. Yet WAD is Najibullah's power base and may not be available for Moscow-sponsored coups. Thus it is impossible to come to a definitive answer on the question of the extent of actual Soviet influence. Obviously tensions exist, and obviously Moscow is determined to exercise tight control even after removal of its troops.

OBSTACLES TO EFFECTIVE SOVIET INFLUENCE

The methods by which Soviet control will be exercised clearly involve the WAD; but they also include an economic program of integration with the USSR, an expanded educational program of Sovietization, the domestication and Sovietization of Afghan religious institutions, internal nationality programs, and the reconstitution of political power by the program of national reconciliation announced in January 1987. All these policies aim to promote movement toward Sovietization, as in postwar Eastern Europe or Khiva and Bukahra after 1920, and all presuppose the structuring of an effective party organization capable of unity and cohesion in this process. But this prospect is far off and very doubtful as well as having been one of the main impediments to effective direct Soviet control over the situation in Afghanistan.

This prospect is far off because the party as a whole has never been able to consolidate its own internal composition let alone command support from the vital bases of Afghan society. In the fall of 1988 it was quite clear that without the massive Soviet intervention, currently being upgraded in the form of high-performance Mig-27s and Scud missiles, slowed down Soviet withdrawal and the political muscle demonstrated in Vorontsov's appointment, the regime would fall apart. The reasons for this are many, but major causes are its refusal to deal with and/or organize the masses, and the endless internecine strife between the Khalq and Parcham wings of the party.

The struggle between these two wings is rooted in the social origin of their former leaders (Babrak Karmal, Nur Mohammad Taraki, and Hafizullah Amin), their strategies for revolutionary socialism in Afghanistan, and since 1979 the very long memories of the outrages perpetrated by each upon the other in their endless battles.[6] The bitterness of these struggles and continual bloodletting among the elite was, in Raja Anwar's opinion, the main cause of the disintegration of the Afghan army in 1980-81.[7] Even in Moscow these rival "gangs" indulged in defenestrations of their rivals.[8] Both wings shared a disdain for the masses that led them to concentrate solely on elite intrigues in Kabul and neglect the real spadework needed to effectuate any policy. In 1978-79 land reform campaigns were always preceded by large propaganda meetings, music, banners, speeches, and slogans. But once the show was over the authorities left for the next campaign to organize more meetings covered by radio and television and nothing was done. Peasants duly concluded that the show, not the reform, was serious. Hence the poor peasants, supposedly the beneficiaries of the reform, were the first to take up arms against the regime.[9] Not only did the regime attempt to steal the masses' "bread," it did not know how to stage effective circuses.

The dire situation of the regime was, of course, well known to the Soviet Union. Soviet television reported in September 1988 that not one of the 32 provinces of Afghanistan was wholly under Kabul's control.[10] In late 1988 the overall situation of the regime continued to deteriorate. Daily rocket firings into Kabul caused definite psychological and political damage to the regime by demonstrating the strength and confidence of the Mujaheddin. Major Abdul Ghaffar Ghopan, who recently defected from Kabul, concurred that the Mujaheddin were able to conduct operations in the towns because the majority of the urban population supports them.[11]

In a speech in October 1988 President Najibullah lashed out at these failures. He flayed his own party's relaxation of efforts after the signing of the Geneva treaty. He admitted, however, that Soviet troops no longer conducted combat operations, leaving the Afghan army to defend the entire country while the number of armed detachments actively opposing the regime doubled in the summer of 1988. Exhorting his followers to action he complained that much time was wasted due to "hollow words"—that is, the persisting disinclination to work with the masses. He went on to observe that

> our work with the opposition is bad. By this I mean the sending of letters and signing of protocols. I believe that each one of us could do a lot of work in this area. Contact could be made with the opposition through the villages and relatives in order to advance our policy. We are expecting further work from the National Front. A new struggle should begin to establish contacts and compromise with the internal and external opposition.[12]

Najibullah also conceded that the PDPA had made few concessions at the district and provincial levels. After a long period of boasting of party successes in numbers of members or supporters among clergy and military that are bald prevarications, like almost all of Kabul's official statements, he came to the sad truth. He admitted that actually little or nothing had been accomplished. Incessant party squabbling has held party members back from doing organizational work. Instead they prefer to stay in Kabul to settle scores. Factionalists (Khalqi or Karmal supporters) have opposed the national reconciliation program, party unity, and policies. Of 9,500 commissions formed to exchange views with party members—an attempt to borrow the spirit of Gorbachev's glasnost—only in 52 did comrades express doubts about the reconciliation program, concealing their views for purposes of obstructing it from within.[13] Moreover, some of these elements have engaged in treason or plotting against Najibullah with the armed forces. The former charge here refers to the Kunduz's commander's abortive efforts to surrender the city to the insurgents.

Thus from 1979, instead of the party being able to penetrate the enemy exclusively, it has destroyed itself and been penetrated by the Mujaheddin.[14] The same holds true for the army officer corps and even more for common recruits. The party picture is so bad that it was also recently reported that Najibullah cannot or will not go abroad for medical treatment of a kidney problem lest he be overthrown. Indeed, he reportedly lost faith in his closest associates.[15] Meanwhile the Mujaheddin's power grows to the degree of forcing the Soviets to make these infusions of heavy weaponry. The Mujaheddin have been able to control Kabul at night and infiltrate to within blocks of Najibullah's residence.[16] North of Kabul, Paghman is half controlled by the rebels and five provincial capitals plus 80 percent of the countryside is in rebel hands. The Soviet engineer at the Salang tunnel told foreign reporters that he stays on at the request (that is, the suffrance) of the rebel leader Massoud.[17]

These developments have apparently only reinforced Najibullah's and Gorbachev's determination to impose a regime capable of doing Moscow's bidding upon Afghanistan. In other words the most recent round of purges of the PDPA represents a continuation of Moscow's quest for a pro-Soviet regime to Kabul. Having failed in battle Moscow still seeks to cheat destiny and arrange a political solution that would retain the PDPA in a position of primacy, regardless of the personalities involved. Najibullah's October 29, 1988, speech is one of the most melodramatic examples of this continuing determination.

Najibullah minced no words, telling all political parties, organizations, and armed groups that they must either cooperate or perish (his term) because the current situation requires that everyone put the common good ahead of his own private interest.[18] Despite this intense call to national reconciliation he made it clear that he would never give up the struggle, nor would the party, even at the price of his life. He claimed that any plan that did not consider

> the reality of the present political system in Afghanistan, that is the PDPA, the government of the Republic of Afghanistan, the Armed Forces, its political allies, social organizations such as youth, women, trade unions and others, will be marked with failure and fraud from the beginning.[19]

Accordingly he launched a purge, coinciding with Soviet Ambassador Vorontsov's arrival in Kabul. About 350 members of the party and 17 Central Committee members were arrested from both Khalq and Parcham factions. This followed many reports of imminent coups against Najibullah.[20]

In Washington this purge was seen as a Soviet effort to oust hard-liners opposed to making a deal with the rebels so that Moscow can impose a coalition upon Afghanistan.[21] In Kabul and Islamabad foreign diplomats and resistance sources interpreted the purges in less earthshaking terms, saying that the police sweeps were designed to prevent Najibullah's opponents from speaking at the Central Committee meetings. Among those arrested were Karmal's half-brother Muhammad Barialay, Karmal's long-time mistress Anahita Ratebzad, and political commissar of the armed forces General Mohammad Yasin Saddiqi. According to local observers these hard-core Parchamites and their associates oppose the withdrawal of Soviet troops. But Khalq forces oppose Najibullah's efforts to bring the Mujaheddin into the coalition because, among other things, he is a Parchamite and not as committed to radical policies. Though the Khalqi dominate the armed forces they apparently have been kept down continually in the government since the 1979 invasion.[22]

Thus it appears that Vorontsov's mandate was to square the same circle as in 1978-79. He is to enhance Soviet influence so that it can impose a coalition upon Afghanistan against the wishes of the two main wings of the PDPA. In the end it probably will not matter since the rebels have made it clear they will not accept either group. But the effort goes on to square this circle and forge at least the illusion of some sort of "third force" that will enable the PDPA and Moscow in time to reassert their hegemony in the area while Moscow disengages its troops. Thus Kabul reportedly sent another emissary to former King Zahir Shah in Rome to persuade him to return home and lend his authority to the regime's program of reconciliation.[23] Simultaneously, reports from Islamabad claimed that Pakistan, the United Nations, and the Soviet Union have stepped up efforts to bring about a political solution that would include Zahir Shah. This would be a reversal of both former Soviet and Pakistani policies. Allegedly, Zahir Shah was willing and ready to visit either Kabul or Peshawar in early 1989 because he was acceptable to both Kabul and Moscow. Though Zahir Shah indicated his unwillingness to play a role while the Muhjaheddin and Afghan government are at loggerheads, it was reported that moderate rebel factions would accept him.[24] This appears to be a rather tenuous solution and one that official rebel spokespeople already dismiss, saying that the king is merely a historical figure with no relevance to the present.

These reports also indicate Najibullah's and Premier Mohammad Hassan Sharq's willingness to step down for Zahir Shah. At the same time it certainly does seem that Moscow is grooming the premier for greater things. Ostensibly a neutral figure, though allegedly a secret KGB agent, Sharq is a perfect figure for the kind of government Moscow seeks to cobble together. He admitted in an October 1988 interview that the public has no confidence in the government, that the PDPA would not fight to retain power in a coalition with the rebels, and that he would resign if any one party tried to hang onto power. The premier stated his willingness to support the king if he could bring an end to the war. However, he ruled out a cessation of Soviet aid and defended the invasion and Soviet aid as being purely defensive responses to official invitations.[25] The Soviets lavished attention on the Afghan premier in the fall of 1988 while silent, or at best pessimistic, about Najibullah's future. Soviet disillusionment led many to speculate that Moscow was seeking to distance itself from Najibullah.[26]

All of the foregoing—the purges, the invocations of Zahir Shah, the supposed reconciliation attempts—are essentially reruns of the same old programs and policies. In 1986-87, the first two years of Najibullah's reign, exactly the same occurred, with purges of the Karmal faction, the Central Committee, the party, the army, and so on. Territorial control shrank to the point where admittedly 92 percent of the army's volunteers were from Kabul, testifying to the shakiness of control elsewhere and the efficiency of regime press gangs in Kabul. By the same token the prominent publicity given in the reconciliation program to support for Islam was as much a feature of Karmal's reign as it is of Najibullah's. One can also make similar statements concerning the regularity of the purges as well.[27]

Thus the reconciliation program is and has been merely a sham. In religion, the regime's professions of support for Islam and Najibullah's supposed religiosity have been belied by the fact that he was seen wearing shoes in the mosque and in his defensive admission to party ideologues that while support for religion was contradictory to scientific socialism, it was a practical necessity. In other words, like Soviet concessions in 1920-21, it was merely a tactical concession to be withdrawn when the time was right. To implement the national reconciliation program, executive organs called Extraordinary Commissions (the original name of the Soviet Cheka, the ancestor of the KGB) were set up. This unfortunate title betrayed the origins and provenance of the program because their ostensibly peaceful role was contradicted by Soviet press reports that a combined Afghan-Soviet offensive against a resistance group took place on "special instructions of the Supreme Extraordinary Commission for National Reconciliation."[28] Nonetheless Najibullah, the regime, and Moscow continue to trumpet the program of national reconciliation and various front groups associated with the PDPA in various power-sharing forms, all of which are fig leaves for the PDPA's continued control.

One reason for the continuation of this policy of fronts and reconciliation in a mixed economy that bends over backward to avoid the "s-word" (socialism) is that through such political solutions Moscow hopes to surmount the Khalq-Parcham rivalry and create a reliably pro-Moscow cadre.[29] Equally plausible is the possibility that the fronts created by this system will enable the regime to plant the ranks of these supposedly non-PDPA groups with WAD agents. There are already several thousand of such agents in WAD, which is heavily saturated with party members who are probably too compromised to accept a coalition or be accepted in one.[30] Selig Harrison consistently invoked a figure of about 375,000 army, secret police, party, and civil service members as a core of support for the regime. More recently John Temple Swing of the Council of Foreign Relations presented a figure of 30,000 in the Sarandoy troops, under the control of the deposed minister of interior and now ambassador to the Soviet Union, Sayed M. Ghulabzoi, and some 35,000 troops of WAD. He also quotes a figure of 350,000 people reported to be on Najibullah's payroll.[31] What is certain, however, is that in lieu of a viable network of public support or party unity, the WAD has become the main arm of the regime in pursuing its most ominous policies of penetrating Afghan society and laying the foundation for its possible ethnic Balkanization. At the same time WAD is a cadet branch of the KGB and is certainly reinforced by several thousand Soviet advisors who will remain once the troops leave.

The regime will have to depend mainly on these elite forces, whose harmony is by no means assured, and the Soviet advisors because the army and the party are divided. Since Ghulabzoi is a Khalq he probably was Najibullah's chief rival and probably owed his place to Soviet insistence on a "bipartisan" regime. Thus there is a possibility for Sarandoy-WAD conflicts. Moreover, the army is rife with demoralization, with well-known instances of betrayal and cooperation with the rebels. One-third of the draftees and one-quarter of the officers regularly desert. Ninety-two percent of recent draftees were from the Kabul area, a sign of profound general disaffection. Finally, executions in the infamous Pul-i-Charkhi prison in Kabul ran about 450 in the first three months of 1988.[32]

THE SOVIETIZATION AND
BALKANIZATION OF AFGHANISTAN

Soviet intentions not to abandon the quest for a communist regime in Kabul are, of course, most visible in the suspension of its troop withdrawals announced in October–November 1988. But this action is not enough nor is it the only way in which Moscow seeks to retain its hold on Afghanistan. Economics, education, and nationality policy within Afghanistan constitute the three main pillars by which Moscow hopes to retain its influence once troops have left. The Geneva Accords were silent on the retention of Soviet advisors, and estimates of the number of these advisors in the armed forces, WAD, economic operations, ministries, and educational offices rise into the tens of thousands. There also are unconfirmed reports of several thousand Soviet Central Asian troops or toughs, specially trained and left behind to meld into Afghan armed forces, leavened throughout those forces to strengthen them against the Mujaheddin or to provide a special corps of potential "elite" forces. In August 1988, Foreign Minister Shevardnadze also announced the completion of a Soviet-inspired long-term program for economic, technical, and trade cooperation between Afghanistan and the USSR until the year 2000.

This program has two goals: reviving the Afghan economy and integrating it still further into the Soviet one. It aims at being a comprehensive blueprint for reviving all sectors of the Afghan economy and organizing joint Soviet-Afghan production projects. The DRA and Soviet government have both repeatedly announced their intention to aid the private sector in its efforts to revive trade and production and this agreement also apparently has this in mind. Shevardnadze emphasized that in this regard the program calls for strengthening traditional forms of border trade and Afghan-Soviet trade along with the introduction of new products and forms of exchange. Afghan personnel (and estimates of the number involved again range into the thousands) will continue to undergo Soviet training, technical and political. Direct ties between Soviet provinces, cities, and republics will also be strengthened as a result of this accord.[33] It should be pointed out that as of the spring of 1988 there already existed 409 of these kinds of economic agreements between Soviet institutions and political entities and Afghan ministries overseeing Afghanistan's economy.

In view of the devastated condition of the economy and its human resources, the Soviet agreements have certain clear objectives in mind that go beyond integrating Afghanistan into Soviet economic structures and plans. First, the agreements constitute a license for the continuing exploitation of mineral and energy resources, in the region adjoining the Soviet border, by means of manipulated terms of trade and pricing agreements. In effect the Soviet exploitation of Afghan resources at below market prices will be used to subsidize the Soviet costs of war so that Afghanistan pays Soviet costs and also bears the costs of being a vast free-fire zone.

Second, the Afghan economy will not be allowed to develop toward balanced production between agriculture and other sectors. Agriculture is devastated, famine is threatening, cities are swollen, and accelerating inflation adds to the burdens. Afghanistan will be dependent on the outside world for foodstuffs and every kind of health care. Soviet provision of these goods will undoubtedly be paid out of Afghan exports, further starving the Afghan economy for hard currency. Human resources will be further subjected to Sovietization in education. The economic basis for detaching northern Afghanistan in name or in fact from the national economy and transferring it to the Soviet one will be completed. Finally the development of Soviet roads and military infrastructural investments, mainly in the north, also ensures the future possibilities for military integration of the area as well.[34]

Soviet policies have now enabled the DRA to make multilateral deals with the Council for Mutual Economic Assistance members, whereas before it could only conclude bilateral agreements. Soviet aid has taken precisely the form of foodstuffs and consumer goods to which its policies have deliberately deprived access, and 75 percent of these goods are distributed by propaganda units of the DRA, and representatives of the WAD or regular police.[35]

Conditions deteriorate shockingly from day to day. One-third of the 1979 population is now a refugee one; and 9 percent of the country has been killed in the war, a higher proportional rate than the Soviet Union's in World War II. Three-quarters of the prewar villages are abandoned or destroyed. Between 10 and 30 million undiscovered mines litter the countryside. Starvation of the rural economy is a growing threat to the indigeneous population as neglect and destruction of the rural ecology and the shortage of labor to work the fields have combined to throw the farm economy into total chaos. Farm production is less than 50 percent of 1978 figures for these reasons and the lack of draft animals. Roads, bridges, schools, and infrastructural resources have been destroyed or bombed, and more than 100,000 skilled professionals have fled the country (no figures exist for the number of professionals killed).

In Kabul one-third of Soviet shipped goods are reportedly stolen. The population there has probably grown to 2 million rather than the official 1.3 million, the natural result of an influx of rural refugees. Much of this population lives in appalling slum conditions, lacking sanitary housing, water, and electric power. Structural breakdowns of the demographic conditions indicate a nation of widows and orphans because the mortality rate of men far exceeds that of women. This in turn entails a breakdown of traditional families and the substitution of bureaucratically organized relief efforts for them. These conditions not only compromise any future hopes for Afghan development, they also to some degree replicate past Russian and Soviet policies in Central Asia after the Tsarist conquest.[36]

The depopulation of the rural population, the heart of anticommunist support, and its relocation in the cities where it becomes available for political mobilization and proletarianization is a sine qua non of continued PDPA or Soviet rule. Thus Kabul's population has tripled since 1978. Since the policies of rural depopulation are a deliberate effort on both the USSR's and DRA's part, it can only be surmised that they have been undertaken with such political and traditional Soviet military ones in mind. Moreover, by equalizing to a greater degree than before the ethnic makeup of the country, the proportion of Pushtuns decreasing from 39 to 22 percent, these policies make it possible to Balkanize the country more easily. The Tajiks now constitute the largest group, with 34 percent of the population, and may be more susceptible to such policies. Soviet annexation of the Wakhan corridor and of its Kirgiz population gives a foretaste of what we might expect. Finally, the ecological consequences of devastation of a semidesert area, depopulation, economic destruction, and mass flight from the countryside are too predictable as to require lengthy analysis. Evidence seems to indicate that those consequences are already making their presence felt.[37]

Soviet educational efforts have replicated earlier efforts of the 1920s to deal with Muslim insurgents (the Basmachi) inside the Soviet Union. A program of orphanages within and without the country, summer camps, university education for politically loyal students, education and indoctrination of thousands per annum in the USSR is functioning, but evidently with little success. This program not only seeks to raise a communist generation, emancipated from influences extraneous to the PDPA's or the Soviet Union's, it also clearly seeks to weaken family and religious ties and substitute state ones instead in true totalitarian fashion. Manipulation of the languages of education also indicate an attempt to foster rising national sentiments among each group so as to lay the groundwork for this potential Balkanization.[38]

Beginning in 1987 the Soviet press for the first time reported the involvement of Uzbek officials in Northern Afghanistan's education programs as a harbinger of these policies. The Soviets also are expanding the role of Central Asian teachers and schools inside Soviet Central Asia to teach Afghanis so that cross-border communication will increase and be made easier.[39] There is also evidence that the DRA is using access to education as a reward for political loyalists, like WAD members or their families, and thus seeks to use access to learning to co-opt adherents.[40] These policies, including creation of state-monitored fronts or unions for writers and for clericoreligious institutions, appear not to have convinced Afghans to join the revolution. Apparently, therefore, Balkanization appears as a potential course of last resort in Moscow's effort to retain influence over Afghanistan.[41]

These efforts at Balkanization of Afghanistan are frequently cited by outside observers (and occasionally by Soviet or Afghan commentators in the most discreet manner) because many of the policies undertaken since 1979 otherwise have no apparent rationale. It should also be noted that these policies consciously harken back to Soviet models. During the 1920s in its struggle against the Basmachi insurgents in Central Asia (a struggle often cited as an analogy to the present one in Afghanistan), Moscow broke up the Central Asian and Caucasian Muslims, creating artificial nationalities or republics and linguistic groups where none had existed in order to Balkanize the area.[42] Not only have Soviet analysts of all stripes utilized the Basmachi analogy in their written analyses, the educational policies adopted for Afghanistan directly replicate those used in the 1920s. Hence the only rational goal of these policies appears to be that Moscow and Kabul are reserving the option of Balkanization if all else fails in order to create the basis either for a deal with Pakistan (a greater Pushtunistan), a Soviet-backed Afghan irredenta, outright annexation by Moscow, or if the regime in Kabul prevails, the basis for threatening Pakistan with the Pushtun and Baluchi cards.

The following phenomena are evident in the Kabul regime's nationality policy. The regime created a Ministry of Tribes and Nationalities modeled upon the old Soviet one of 1917-24. Its purpose is to endow each nationality with the means of achieving "equality," through their own language materials, publications, schools, and, in the north, the most developed area economically and the richest in terms of resources, a separate administration. This ministry was headed, first of all, by Najibullah and is thus undoubtedly now an auxiliary of the secret police.[43]

By giving each nationality its own media for cultural self-expression, Kabul and Moscow have repudiated the Pushtun first policy of the Afghan dynasty, which sought to "Afghanize" the country around the Pushtun issue. They have also effectively created a host of subnational "nationalisms" that can be used to detach or divide parts of Afghanistan and Pakistan from each other and prompt a redrawing of boundaries. There is an enormous and constant interpenetration of Afghanistan by Soviet Central Asian cadres and professionals whose purpose is clearly to cement ties of ethnic affiliation with Soviet Muslims. Many of these assemblies or meetings decry the political demarcation of the Oxus River, the interstate boundary with the USSR, as an artificial impediment to the unity of the peoples.[44] At the same time the 1985 Loya Jirga—an assembly of all tribes and groups and pre-1978 the highest authority in Afghanistan—was convened from Pushtun tribes on both sides of the Durand line. At this conclave Babrak Karmal explicitly advocated their reunification under Afghan sovereignty.[45]

The creation of a separate administration in northern Afghanistan led by deputy Prime Minister Mihanparast before 1988 and since March 1988 by Najibullah Masir, and of a separate military command led by General Juma Isak, certainly signifies the importance of this resource-rich and contiguous area to Soviet Central Asia. The Central Asian influence is most noticeable here as are efforts to bring together all available media in a coordinated campaign to pacify the area and enhance its regional identity and ties to Central Asia. The extent of this can be seen in the fact that the regional Communist Party, the Setam Milli, is separate from the Khalqi and Parcham factions of the PDPA. All in all, it would appear that the option to Balkanize is well enough developed to be employed should Soviet strategic calculations so ordain.[46] Culturally, administratively, militarily, organizationally, and economically northern Afghanistan has attained a semblance of a separate identity that can be invoked for many future purposes.

CONCLUSION

Just prior to the completion of Soviet troop withdrawals in February 1989, the Soviet government offered a pessimistic assessment of the future of the Afghan government. Soviet Foreign Ministry spokesman Gennadi I. Gerasimov said that the guerrillas were "massing" around Kabul in preparation for the onslaught once Soviet troops were gone. He made no claim for the ability of the Kabul regime to survive but rather noted how many Afghan army posts had fallen in recent days and the assault on the city of Kandashar. The effect of Gerasimov's comments was to give the impression that Moscow was washing its hands of the whole affair. It was left to the Afghan ambassador, Mr. Ghulabzoi, to predict the survival of the regime. Bolstered by the transfer of military equipment and food, he said that the government forces were strengthened and concluded: "All patriotic forces will defend the country, and we will win."[47]

By the summer of 1989, the dire prediction of early months had not been fulfilled. Due both to the skill of President Najibullah and the military failures of the Mujaheddin, the Kabul regime appeared stronger. The departure of the Soviets left the government with a life-or-death situation that has strengthened the resolve of the regime and its armed forces. Najibullah has also played on the divisions among the Mujaheddin by allowing guerrilla commanders to continue running their own fiefdoms as long as they do not trouble the government. The effect of his offer has been to further weaken the tenuous bonds of the Mujaheddin organization by creating disincentives to fight. Some of the people surrounding the president have concluded that, short of an outright guerrilla victory, the only things that could end his tenure would be Soviet pressure and the defection of his supporters.[48]

A viable peace proposal from the Mujaheddin and its supporters might be the quickest way to bring down the Kabul regime. However, the Mujaheddin remain divided and unable to agree on any kind of future agenda. Despite their resolve not to lose, the Kabul regime cannot win as long as the Mujaheddin are supplied from the outside.

But the failure of the guerrillas to capture Jalalabad and the diminishing supply of Stinger antiaircraft missiles make the Mujaheddin more vulnerable and victory less certain. A neutralized regime, headed by ex-King Zahir Shah and embracing the PDPA and the Mujaheddin, appears to command no support among the guerrillas or among members of the Khalqi faction of the regime who remain deeply antagonistic to the old status quo and presumably to the Russians for suggesting it. The Khalqi faction seeks to continue the fighting to the end, and by stepping up their attacks on Kabul, the guerrillas appear to be seeking the same end.[49]

The reforms associated with glasnost and perestroika in the USSR presuppose a unified political elite in regard to questions of broad policy and a deepening dialogue with the intelligentsia and the politically educated circles of the country. So too in Afghanistan, genuine national reconciliation presupposes a legitimate regime that is strong enough to conduct a meaningful dialogue among its elites and with the people. The bitter divisions among the regime that have never been forgotten, the insecurity of the leadership and resulting policy divisions, and the socioeconomic devastation all heavily mortgage the future of the country.

Moscow has influence in that it can compel regime members to proclaim policies at variance with their private perspectives. On the other hand it clearly cannot compel action to implement these policies outside a narrow geographical and political compass because the regime is both so divided and so bankrupt. By invading, Moscow assumed responsibility for preserving the regime and still seeks some means of Sovietizing at least a part of Afghanistan, either geographically or politically. Its conspicuous failure to achieve those goals to date has not fully sunk in as recent actions indicate.

In many ways Afghanistan is Moscow's Vietnam. For example, the belief that one need only get rid of obstacles at the top—like Amin in 1979, Karmal in 1985–86, and the dissidents in the fall of 1988—to achieve a political solution was also rife in Vietnam. Soviet officials, like Americans before them, are experiencing the fact that direct intervention in third-party civil wars only engenders both partners' demoralization. That process is evident both in the stories of veterans in the USSR and in the revelations of cowardice and betrayal by Afghan communists and officers.[50]

Ultimately Soviet leverage did not suffice. In withdrawing its troops, Moscow is finding its leverage declining even as it refuses to admit this by still seeking to force a solution upon Afghanistan. Soviet leaders, not to mention the PDPA, apparently still have not fully grasped Bismarck's observation, "woe to the statesman whose reasons for getting out of a war are not the same as for getting in." Moscow's war to defend the 1978 coup and abortive revolution exemplifies his insight. Moscow ironically banks on a return to the monarchy it destroyed, because it and the PDPA have made it virtually certain that neither socialism nor glasnost can flourish there. If peace comes in the foreseeable future it will only be because like Tacitus' Romans, "they made a desert and called it peace."

NOTES

The views expressed here do not in any way represent those of the U.S. Air Force, Department of Defense, or any agency of the U.S. government.

1. Alvin Z. Rubinstein, *Red Star on the Nile: The Soviet-Egyptian Influence Relationship Since the June 1967 War* (Princeton, NJ: Princeton University Press, 1977), pp. xvi–xxiii, discusses the nature and measurement of influence as does Alvin Z. Rubinstein ed., *Soviet and Chinese Influence in the Third World* (New York: Praeger Publishers, 1975), pp. 10-15.

2. Stephen Blank, "Soviet Russia and Low Intensity Conflict in Central Asia: Three Case Studies" in *Low Intensity Conflict in the Third World*, eds. Lewis Ware et al. (Maxwell Air Force Base, AL: Air University Press, 1988), pp. 51-74.

3. M. Nazif Shahrani and Robert Canfield, eds., *Revolutions and Rebellions in Afghanistan: Anthropological Perspectives* (Berkeley: Institute of International Studies, University of California, 1984).

4. For a discussion of Karmal's policies and failures, see Henry Bradsher, "Stagnation and Change in Afghanistan," *Journal of South Asian and Middle Eastern Studies* 10 (Fall 1986): 1-35.

5. Selig S. Harrison, "Inside the Afghan Talks," *Foreign Policy* 72 (Fall 1988): 31-60.

6. Raja Anwar, *The Tragedy of Afghanistan: A First-Hand Account* (London: Verso Books, 1988), pp. 39-229; Anthony Arnold, *Afghanistan's Two Party Communism: Parcham and Khalq* (Stanford, CA: Hoover Institution Press, 1983), pp. 23-51.

7. Anwar, *The Tragedy*, pp. 209-218.

8. J. Bruce Amstutz, *Afghanistan: The First Five Years of Soviet Occupation* (Washington, D.C.: National Defense University Press, 1986), pp. 54, 79-80.

9. Sayd B. Majrooh, "The Russian Intervention in Afghanistan: The Economic War," *Central Asian Survey* 4, no. 4 (1985): 104-105.

10. *Daily Report-Soviet Union* (Foreign Broadcast Information Service, hereafter FBIS), September 26, 1988, p. 37.

11. *Daily Report-South Asia* (FBIS) October 21, 1988, p. 39.
12. *Daily Report-South Asia* (FBIS) October 24, 1988, p. 51.
13. Ibid., p. 55.
14. For example, see *Daily Report-South Asia* (FBIS) August 1, 1988, p. 51.
15. *Daily Report-South Asia* (FBIS) October 21, 1988, p. 39.
16. "Kabul Defenders Face a Deadly Nibbling," *Boston Globe*, October 3, 1988, p. 1.
17. "In Vodka Veritas," *The Economist*, October 8, 1988, p. 42.
18. *Daily Report-South Asia* (FBIS) October 31, 1988, p. 57.
19. Ibid., p. 60.
20. Richard Beeson, "Soviets Out to Purge Afghan Hard-Liners," *Washington Times*, October 26, 1988, p. 1.
21. Elaine Sciolino, "U.S. Says Soviets Have Deployed New Attack Jets in Afghanistan," *New York Times*, October 30, 1988, pp. 1, 4.
22. Barbara Crossette, "Afghan Leadership Reported at Odds," *New York Times*, October 19, 1988, p. 3.
23. *Daily Report-South Asia* (FBIS) October 20, 1988, pp. 50-51.
24. *Daily Report-South Asia* (FBIS) October 31, 1988, p. 61.
25. *Daily Report-South Asia* (FBIS), October 13, 1988, p. 53.
26. Robert Pear, "U.S. and Afghan Guerrillas Debate New Raids," *New York Times*, September 25, 1988, Section I, p. 5; "Comradely Prod in the Ribs," *The Economist*, November 19, 1988, p. 36.
27. Anthony Arnold, "Afghanistan," in *Yearbook on International Communist Affairs, 1988*, ed. Richard F. Staar (Stanford, CA: Hoover Institution Press, 1988), pp. 394-399.
28. Ibid., pp. 398-399.
29. Edward Girardet, "Russia's War in Afghanistan," *Central Asian Survey* 2, no. 1 (July 1983): 94.
30. Steven Galster, "Rivalry and Reconciliation in Afghanistan: What Prospects for the Accords?" *Third World Quarterly* 10 (October 1988): 1535.
31. Selig S. Harrison, "Containment and the Soviet Union in Afghanistan," in *Containment: Concept and Policy*, eds. Terry L. Deibel and John Lewis Gaddis (Washington, D.C.: National Defense University Press, 1986), p. 465; John Temple Swing, "Afghanistan After the Accords: A Report from Kabul," *Critical Issues* (Council on Foreign Relations) 6 (1988): 9-10 and 21-22.
32. Swing, "Afghanistan After the Accords," p. 9.
33. Interview with Soviet Foreign Minister Shevardnadze by the Bakhtar News Agency, in *Daily Report-Soviet Union* (FBIS) August 9, 1988, pp. 16-19.
34. M. Siddieq Noorzoy, "Long-Term Soviet Economic Interests and Policies in Afghanistan" and John F. Shroder and Abdul Tawab Assifi, "Afghan Mineral Resources and Soviet Exploitation," in *Afghanistan: The Great Game Revisited*, ed. Roseanne Klass (New York: Freedom House, 1987), pp. 71-96 and 97-134, respectively.
35. Arnold, "Afghanistan," p. 399.

36. Edward Girardet, "Afghans Find War Brutal, but Gain New Sense of Nationhood," *Christian Science Monitor*, October 24, 1988, pp. 1, 12; *Daily Report-Soviet Union* (FBIS) September 28, 1988, p. 35; Marek Silwinski, "Afghanistan 1978-87: War, Democracy, and Society," *Central Asian Survey*, Incidental Papers Series, 6 (May 1988).

37. Ibid.

38. U.S. Department of State, Bureau of Intelligence and Research, "Afghanistan and Soviet Nationalities," *Soviet Nationalities Survey* 14 (Washington, D.C.: Government Printing Office, March 1, 1988), pp. 2-7.

38. Ibid., pp. 7-9.

40. B. Almqvist, "The Afghan War in 1983: Strengthened Resistance Versus Soviet 'Nazi Tactics,'" *Central Asian Survey* 4 (1984): 41.

41. Chantal Lobato, "Islam in Kabul: The Religious Politics of Babrak Karmal," *Central Asian Survey* 4, no. 4 (1985): 111-120; Nancy Hatch Dupree, "The Conscription of Afghan Writers: An Aborted Experiment in Socialist Realism," *Central Asian Survey* 4 (1985): 69-87, *Soviet Nationalities Survey*, passim.

42. Stephen Blank, *Stalin's Commissariat of Nationalities: The Sorcerer as Apprentice, 1917-1924* (DeKalb: Northern Illinois University Press, forthcoming), chapter 9.

43. A. Rasul Amin, "A General Reflection of the Stealthy Sovietization of Afghanistan," *Central Asian Survey* 3, no. 1 (1984): 58-61.

44. A. Rasul Amin and Nazeem Rizvi, "Sovietization of Afghanistan," *Strategic Studies* (Islamabad) 11 (Summer 1988): 39-40.

45. Blank, "Soviet Russia," p. 67.

46. Joseph Newman, Jr., "The Future of Northern Afghanistan," *Asian Survey* 38 (July 1988): 729-739.

47. John F. Burns, "Soviets Are Glum About Kabul's Future," *New York Times*, February 10, 1989, p. 6.

48. "How Nice To Find A Third Way," *The Economist*, July 8, 1989, p. 32.

49. Ibid.; John F. Burns, "Kabul Car Bomb Laid To Rebels Kills 9," *New York Times*, July 16, 1989, p. 3.

50. *Daily Report-South Asia* (FBIS), September 2, 1988, p. 41.

CHAPTER 6

Gorbachev and the Korean Issue

ROY U.T. KIM

Profound changes are afoot in the geopolitical landscape in Northeast Asia since Mikhail Gorbachev's coming to power in March 1985. Confronted with unprecedented economic stagnation, widespread social apathy, and a widening technological lag vis-à-vis the prosperous Pacific Basin, Gorbachev has undertaken the most far-reaching revamping of the Soviet system in over half a century. Compared with his predecessors' diplomatic stagnation, Gorbachev's diplomatic initiatives have rekindled the nearly forgotten Korean issue. Not only has he suggested a multilateral conference to reduce military confrontation in the Korean peninsula, but he has also indicated possibilities of establishing economic ties with South Korea (ROK). Mindful of past obligations, Gorbachev perhaps will consider visiting Pyongyang and also inviting possible future North Korean leaders to the Soviet Union.

Equally profound changes have been taking place in Seoul. Under Roh Tae Woo, the first president in modern South Korean history who assumed the presidency peacefully, Seoul has ushered in a new era of expanding contacts with Socialist states, including Beijing, Moscow, and Pyongyang. Responding positively to Gorbachev's September 17, 1988, Krasnoyarsk suggestion, Roh proposed, in his October 18, 1988 UN speech, a multilateral conference among the United States, the Soviet Union, China, Japan, and the two Koreas.

Wearied by three decades of bickering since the end of the Korean War in 1953, the Soviet Union, like the other surrounding powers, has been fatigued and irritated with the continuing stalemate between the two Koreas. Yet the Korean peninsula is the focal point in Northeast Asia where the vital interests of the world's military and economic powers intersect. For this reason, Gorbachev appears to have accorded a very high priority to resolving the Korean regional conflict.

Soviet participation in the 1988 Seoul Olympics initiated the change. More than 6,000 Soviets attended the 1988 Games, the largest Soviet presence in South Korea since 1945, when the Red Army, along with U.S. forces, liberated Korea from 35 years of Japanese colonialism. Five 10,000-ton-class Soviet tourist ships were allowed port calls in Pusan and Inchon. Soviet Aeroflots were permitted to land in Seoul. More significantly, a team of Soviet consular officers stayed at the Walker Hill Hotel to serve the visiting Soviets during the games. In short, the Seoul Olympics became an important catalyst in thawing Moscow-Seoul relations.

What is, then, the nature of Gorbachev's initiatives to resolve the regional conflict in the Korean peninsula? How have the two Koreas responded to them? How have Gorbachev's challenges affected the dialogue between Seoul and Pyongyang? What are the problems and prospects for Gorbachev's initiatives to resolve the regional conflict in the Korean peninsula?

The basic purpose of this chapter is to delineate Gorbachev's basic dilemma in the Korean peninsula—that is, reconciling Moscow's obligations to North Korea with the fresh opportunities in South Korea, within the context of Soviet relations with China, Japan, and the United States. The Soviet obligations result largely from perceived mutual interests within the socialist community; whereas the fresh opportunities arise from South Korea, a newly emerging economic entity in the Pacific. Gorbachev declared in his July 1986 Vladivostok speech that "we must rid outselves of the burden of the past and search for new approaches, guided by responsibility for the present and future, if we are to move toward their solution."[1] As will be shown later, strikingly similar drastic changes abound in Moscow and Seoul. In contrast, increasing diversities seem to be appearing between Moscow and Pyongyang. If Gorbachev's initiatives toward the Korean peninsula prove to be successful, they will have a profound impact upon the entire geopolitical landscape in East Asia. Moscow then will be able to gain a favorable position among the four major surrounding powers, for having successfully reduced tension between the two Koreas.

PERESTROIKA IN MOSCOW AND SEOUL

The essentially stagnated Soviet economy has encouraged major changes in Soviet foreign policy.[2] In contrast, Seoul's increasing economic strength and accompanying efforts for political self-reliance appear to be influencing its foreign policy reorientations. For understandable reasons, Gorbachev's foreign policy perestroika has attracted more worldwide media attention than Roh's *buk-bang oae-kyo* (northern diplomacy). Although for different reasons to be sure, perestroika in Moscow and Seoul have striking similarities.

No other Soviet leader in modern times inherited as many serious internal and external problems as Gorbachev. Improving a troubled national economy, he admitted, "is our most important, top-priority task."[3] The Soviet leader candidly blamed the urgency of the task on Moscow's own political short-sightedness, deficiencies, and lack of managerial skills. In his book, Gorbachev tells us:

Perestroika is an urgent necessity arising from the profound processes of development in our socialist society. This society is ripe for change. It has long been yearning for it. Any delay in beginning perestroika could have led to an exacerbated internal situation in the near future, which, to put it bluntly, would have been fraught with serious social, economic and political crises.[4]

Gorbachev, in other words, did not have any other alternatives.[5] Gorbachev's chief economic adviser, Abel Aganbegyan, suggests that at the root of Gorbachev's new economic strategy lies the concept of *uskorienie*, the acceleration of social and economic development in contrast to the tendency of *zamedlenie*, the slowdown of development of the last 15 years.[6] Gorbachev's economic goal is to accelerate the Soviet economic development via innovative activity, economic institutions, and, most important, changes in the mentality of the population concerning the economy and society.[7] For this purpose, Gorbachev, very decisively, broke away from the legacies of Stalin and Brezhnev and firmly established his own "new political thinking."

The Soviet Union should, in theory, be ripe for the sort of modern economic miracle performed since 1945 by West Germany, Japan, and South Korea. It is vastly richer in raw materials than any of those countries. More important, it has a highly educated work force, including, as official statistics claim, 1.5 million scientists, one-quarter of the world's total. Moscow also claims that it has nearly 18 million bureaucrats, more than South Korea's entire working population. More than anybody else, these Soviet bureaucrats stifle almost all Soviet initiatives. Gorbachev faces inertia and the archaic industrial structure acquired by 60 years of socialist central planning.

A most vivid failure of Soviet economy is in the Soviet Far East. Despite heavy investment, a prominent Soviet economist from Khabarovsk, Paval Minakir, readily admits that the main products of the region, largely raw materials, such as coal, gold, petroleum, and timber, have not been selling well. The profit margin has been eliminated, because their prices have been declining worldwide and because wages are much higher in the Far East than elsewhere in the Soviet Union. Soviet Far Eastern economic stagnation appears much more acute when compared with surrounding regions' prosperous economic development.[8] Confronted with these economic crises, Gorbachev has been attempting to replace the Stalinist planned economy with a market economy.

In contrast, Seoul has gone from poverty to budding economic power in the short span of less than three decades. Within a generation, South Koreans have moved from rice paddies and farmhouses to factories and modern apartments. The economy has grown by 8 percent a year since 1958, with real per capita GNP six times what it was then. The wealth is spread relatively evenly. South Korea has one of the most equal income distributions of any modern country at its level of development, and a young South Korean has a good chance of getting a higher education.[9] The newest game in Seoul since the Olympics has been activating global market diversification.

This unprecedented economic prosperity has enabled Seoul to initiate political democracy. This maturing political democracy was clearly shown by two recent elections. They were based on Roh's June 29, 1987, eight-point plan of political reform. South Koreans gave him the nod of legitimacy at the polls on December 16, 1987, but gave him only 36 percent of the vote to remind him that it was a qualified nod—a point they sharply reiterated when they removed Roh's governing Democratic Justice Party's overall majority in the National Assembly elections held in April 1988. These elections have forced Seoul's ruling elites to reduce their monopoly of power. Workers are flexing newly won powers of unionism by demanding a bigger share of the economic miracle they wrought. The process of democratization can still be checked. In fact, some observers in Seoul feared, perhaps somewhat prematurely, that the Roh administration would have to tighten up the screws economically, politically, and socially, particularly after the Olympics.[10]

There is no question that South Korea is a nation coming of age. A booming, liberalizing economy has created an independent-minded and extraordinarily well-educated middle class. South Korea is now the 17th largest economy in the market-economies of the world and the 12th largest trading nation. In 1987 Seoul's exports rose 36 percent, real growth was 12 percent, and unemployment stayed low at 2.2 percent.[11] Lately South Koreans, laden with trade surplus, have emerged as international lenders.[12] South Koreans are savoring something new. Throughout history, their peninsula has been a battleground for the great powers—China, Japan, Russia, and the United States. Now ordinary South Koreans hold their destiny in their own hands as never before. The growing Korean sense of pride and nationalism is expressed openly as resentment of Japan and the United States—powers that dominated Korea in the modern era. With their democratization and economic power, Koreans no longer want to be victims of Japanese colonialism and American cold-war geopolitics.

Striking similarities abound between Moscow and Seoul in their efforts to break away from the past. Roh has appeared somewhat less decisive and slower than Gorbachev, as he seems influenced by what the late Korean scholar Hahm Pyong-choon characterized as the Confucian ethical virtue of *li* (propriety)[13] and the military establishment. Yet for Koreans, the leap from an authoritarian regime to a no-holds-barred public investigation by the National Assembly in a little over a year and a half is no less significant than what is taking place in the Soviet Union. No wonder, Seoul's day and night drama on live TV was as attentively watched in Moscow as the Seoul Olympics. Needless to say, processes of perestroika in Moscow and Seoul are far from over.

POTENTIAL MUTUAL INTERESTS: MOSCOW AND SEOUL

Economically Moscow and Seoul have much to gain from each other. To paraphrase Thucydides, identity of interests is the surest way for improving relations. Moscow has been noticing South Korea maturing economically and politically. Among the four newly industrializing countries (NICs) in the Pacific, Moscow considers Seoul a most suitable partner for mutually beneficial economic relations. Having initiated economic diplomacy in his Vladivostok speech in

July 1986, Gorbachev, as noted above, has proposed to South Korea the establishment of economic ties. Confronted with a stagnated economy at home, he cannot possibly afford to miss the fast-moving Pacific economic train, and he knows South Korea is an important part of it. Gorbachev wants to invite in foreign capital and high technology to cure his seriously ill Soviet economy. South Korean capital and technology are readily available. Besides geographical proximity, South Korea, as viewed from the Soviet Union, is not only a rapidly growing market for raw materials from Siberia, but also an ideal source of consumer goods, parts, technology, managerial expertise, and even a source of badly needed capital. Compared with Japan, Soviet economists openly claim that South Korea's products are much more readily available at a competitive price.[14]

In March 1988 Moscow established the Soviet National Committee for Asia-Pacific Economic Cooperation (SOVNAPEC). Representing academic, business, and government organizations, it wants to be active in the Pacific Economic Cooperation Conference (PECC)[15] where South Korea has been a standing committee member since its foundation. At the PECC's 6th General Meeting, held in Osaka, Japan, in May 1988, SOVNAPEC's chairman Yevgeni Primakov said that Moscow is seriously interested in joining PECC. Pledging close cooperation with PECC, he pleaded for advice and assistance to be an active part of the organization.[16]

South Korean multinationals, *jaebols*, have been keenly interested in global market diversification. They have been looking for new markets in Eastern Europe, China, and the Soviet Union at a time when they see Western trading partners erecting protectionist walls. The expanding South Korean economy needs abundant natural resources from Siberia. Yet Seoul's business executives seriously doubt how they can profit from their investment in the Soviet Union until the Soviet ruble becomes internationally convertible. They are also well aware that, unlike China, there is a serious shortage of labor in the Soviet Far East. Korean business leaders also know that their investment in the Soviet Union can be more profitable than in China, given the Soviet Union's substantially higher per capita income than China's.

Seoul has been seeking trade with Moscow even before Gorbachev's Vladivostok initiative in July 1986. During a visit to Helsinki in May 1979, then South Korean Foreign Minister Pak Dong-jin signed an agreement pledging mutual assistance for private businessmen in exporting South Korean products to the Soviet Union and Eastern Europe. Indirect Moscow-Seoul trade was estimated at about $20 million in 1978, with Moscow importing electronics, textiles, and machinery and exporting coal and timber.[17] For lack of diplomatic relations, most of the Soviet-South Korean trade has been indirect, using Eastern Europe, Hong Kong, Japan, and Singapore. With the increasing volume of exchange, they have begun trading directly, using Nakhodka-Vostochnyy near Vladivostok and the Korean port of Pusan, but still relying on third-countries' ships. Coal and timber from the Soviet Far East arrive in South Korea. The Soviets initially rejected Seoul's request that its ships be admitted to Soviet Far Eastern ports. South Korean goods since 1977 have been shipped on third-country vessels to those ports for transshipment to Europe on the Trans-Siberian Railway. Moscow and Seoul have started using Japan and Great Britain as links for telephone calls.[18] It is generally assumed, though the exact figure is difficult to obtain, the total volume of Moscow-Seoul trade ranged from $240 million to $1 billion in 1987.[19] Several major Korean businesses, including Daewoo, Sunkyong, Jin-do, and Lucky Star, have been directly trading with the Soviet Union.

The Soviet Light Industry Ministry, in a joint venture with Seoul's global fur dealer Jindo, is expected to produce $20 million worth of fur garments each year. For the first time, three South Korean companies (Goldstar, Samsung, and Daewoo) participated in an exhibition of audiovisual electronics in Leningrad.[20] Already 15 percent of Daewoo's trade turnover is reported to be with socialist countries.[21] Major construction projects in the Soviet Union (hotels, sports complex, and others) are under serious negotiations with several of South Korea's major industries.

Most significantly, Moscow and Seoul exchanged a trade memorandum on October 15, 1988. Involving the Soviet Chamber of Commerce and the Korea Trade Promotion Corporation (KOTRA), this semiofficial trade agreement has pledged each party to assist in establishing trade offices in both countries early in 1989. While the details of the memorandum were not immediately known, Seoul's active participation in Siberian development was widely anticipated with a scheduled visit to Moscow in December 1988 by KOTRA's president Sun-ki Lee.[22]

Politically also, Moscow and Seoul have much to gain. Both want to end the protracted confrontation between the two Koreas. To facilitate internal economic development, Moscow badly needs external stability, particularly in the Pacific region. Gorbachev clearly indicated this in his Krasnoyarsk speech in September 1988. With this in mind, the Soviet leader proposed that the Soviet Union, China, Japan, and the two Koreas discuss ways of "freezing and proportionate reduction of naval and air forces" between the two Koreas.[23] The Soviet Union, meanwhile, reportedly has cut back its naval activities, though not the size of its fleet, in the Pacific by 50 percent in the year that ended April 1988.[24] Gorbachev's well-timed, bold initiative, on the eve of the opening of the Seoul Olympics, maximized its political impact, clearly indicating that the Soviet Union intends to take the lead in shaping the new relationships expected to evolve in the Asia-Pacific region out of the increased fluidity of affairs on the Korean peninsula.

Seoul reacted positively. Gorbachev's Krasnoyarsk speech was extensively reported in the South Korean media. A lengthy editorial in the *Dong-A Ilbo*, the largest circulating newspaper in South Korea, welcomed Gorbachev's initiative to reduce military tensions and improve relations within the Pacific region. It echoed equally positive responses from Beijing and somewhat less positive response from Tokyo.[25] Young Sam Kim, president of the opposition Reunification and Democratic Party, observed, in his interview with the Soviet journal *New Times*, that "Gorbachev's proposals will enhance mutual interests between the Soviet Union and South Korea as they are highly realistic."[26]

Perhaps the most positive response was expressed by President Roh himself in his UN speech on October 18, 1988. In the first major address by the ROK president to the UN General Assembly, Roh called for a consultative conference among the United States, the USSR, China, Japan, and the two Koreas "to lay a solid foundation for durable peace and prosperity in Northeast Asia."[27] Most of the address, in fact, was devoted to a call for improving relations between the two Koreas and to a reiteration of the reconciliation offer he made to North Korea in July 1988.

Seoul, too, has much to gain politically. After decades without any relations with the socialist world, the new frontier for emerging South Korea is diplomatic and political. Roh's "northern diplomacy," actively encouraged by Washington, seeks to improve relations with Beijing, Moscow, and Pyongyang. Pressured by persistent domestic calls for better ties with Pyongyang, Seoul is making its most serious effort yet to improve relations with its northern neighbor. The tide for North-South Korean détente, though at times appearing rather precarious, gets stronger. Moscow sees an opportunity to lessen its costly obligations to Pyongyang through improved relations with Seoul. If tensions along the demilitarized zone decrease, the USSR could conceivably gain the upper hand in the Korean peninsula vis-à-vis Beijing, Tokyo, and Washington. Already Moscow has the most leverage with Pyongyang, even without any Soviet military presence. Thus if Gorbachev's initiatives prove successful, they will augur a profound enhancement of Soviet posture in the Korean peninsula. This may also cause a profound change in South Korea's relationship with the United States, as we shall discuss later.

These reasons for Seoul's Soviet euphoria were clearly demonstrated by the enthusiastic reception for the Bolshoi Ballet's first performance in Seoul. When the Soviet team headed for home from the successful Olympics, it took along 36 Korean TV sets, seven minibuses, four large buses, four cars, and one photocopying machine, all gifts of Daewoo Corp.[28] These have been the more visible fruits of the improved Moscow-Seoul relations. Yet despite the progress, there are some nagging old problems.

TROUBLED OLD TIES

Old habits die hard. While the world of confrontation and conflict is giving way to a world of détente, the legacy of the cold war still lingers on in the Korean peninsula. As part of the cold war legacy, Moscow still has burdensome political obligations toward Pyongyang, and Washington provides security for Seoul. So long as Moscow honors this pledge, Washington has to maintain close military-security ties with Seoul, though relations between Moscow and Washington have been markedly improved under Gorbachev. While the emerging Moscow-Washington and Moscow-Seoul détentes may be necessary, they may not be sufficient enough to completely liquidate the cold war between Pyongyang and Seoul.

Yet the Soviet leader appears determined to tackle the Korean problem "as a dictate of our time."[29] With this in mind, Gorbachev and Reagan reportedly discussed the Korean peninsula situation during their Moscow summit, May 29-June 1, 1988.[30] In a joint statement, they "reaffirmed their intention to continue U.S.-Soviet discussions at all levels aimed at helping parties to regional conflicts find peaceful solutions which advance their independence, freedom, and security."[31] For this purpose, high-ranking representatives of Moscow and Washington met in Paris early in October 1988. Soviet Deputy Foreign Minister Igor A. Rogachev and U.S. Assistant Secretary of State for East Asian and Pacific Affairs Gaston J. Sigur, after discussing ways and means to reduce tension in the Korean peninsula, reportedly stressed "the importance of direct dialogue between Pyongyang and Seoul."[32] While welcoming the improving economic relations between Moscow and Seoul, Sigur allegedly requested Rogachev to ask Pyongyang to be more forthcoming in its dialogue with Seoul. Yet in all probability, neither Moscow nor Washington can readily influence Pyongyang and Seoul as in the past. Thus the old ties, though still in existence, appear to be getting rather thin.

To be sure, Moscow and Pyongyang are bound by mutual interests and obligations. Yet they share neither a common heritage nor common perceptions. The forces dividing them increasingly seem to be as strong as those uniting them. Although the alliance can be maintained for a time, it may be gradually diminished by forces beyond their control. Their ties cannot be described other than as a marriage of convenience and necessity. Certainly no love is lost between them. In all probability, the Soviets realize the practical limitations of how much they can influence Pyongyang's behavior and vice versa. Despite the scope of the cumulative Soviet investment in North Korea, the political payoff, from Moscow's perspective, has been relatively marginal and certainly not commensurate. At best the Moscow-Pyongyang relationship could be described as "bittersweet."

How does Gorbachev perceive the North Korean leadership? How will Gorbachev's 20-year age differential with Kim Il Sung affect their relations? In 1950 when the Korean War began, Gorbachev was only in his first year at Moscow State University. From his student days, Gorbachev is said to have developed a suspicion and dislike of Stalinism. Seen from Gorbachev's perspective, Kim, the oldest ruling communist leader, may be perceived as a symbol of Stalinism—the very antithesis of glasnost and perestroika. From Kim's perspective, on the other hand, Gorbachev, though bright and intelligent, must appear highly inexperienced, if daring.

At their first public meeting in Moscow in 1986, Gorbachev was willing to recognize Kim as a prominent and experienced figure in the communist movement. Gorbachev said that "we are convinced that the interests of all Asian states converge on the rejection of neo-globalism, great-power chauvinism and any efforts to force peoples to join military blocs or groupings."[33] He went on to assure his guest that "no one has the right to order peoples around, impose his will on others, or delineate the world map into one's sphere of interest." Yet perhaps responding to Kim's request for economic assistance for Pyongyang's seven-year economic plan, but specifically referring to internal Soviet economic conditions, Gorbachev said to Kim: "you are aware of all the difficulties involved in dealing with the task confronting us." What to do with this given situation? Gorbachev suggested that "each and every one of us [meaning both sides separately] will have to work hard, vigorously and conscientiously . . . as we have a mission to elevate our socialist economic system to a new level."[34] Finally the Soviet leader offered his sympathy by saying that the Soviet people have "profound respect for the Korean people, their hard-working and energetic character and their loyalty to the great cause of the reunification of their homeland."

Gorbachev's message to Kim reflected Moscow's drive to get rid of the burden of the past. In practical terms, it implies that each socialist state is responsible for its own economic development and entitled to a foreign policy based on complete independence. This shift has been clearly and consistently reflected in Gorbachev's major pronouncements, including such key documents as the new CPSU program published in October 1985, Gorbachev's own report to the 27th Party Congress in February 1986, in his Vladivostok speech of July 1986, in his book *Perestroika*, and in his lengthy speech at the 19th All-Union Conference of the CPSU, June 28, 1988.[35] Reporting on progress in implementing the decisions of the 27th Party Congress at the 19th Party Conference the general secretary declared: "Together with our [socialist] friends . . . we have endeavored . . . to rid the internationalist essence of our relations of the sediment that accumulated on them in the past." Indeed, gone are the generous Soviet offers of economic and military assistance for the Third World countries. Instead the new Gorbachevian posture seems to emphasize that while the Soviet Union "has profound sympathy" (as Gorbachev expressed to Kim) for the aspirations of the Third World countries, the Third World socialist countries "must develop their own economies mainly through their own efforts." In other words, Moscow could not and would not provide economic and military assistance beyond its limited resources.[36] Thus the first priority Gorbachev stresses is the Soviet Union's own internal development, and any external economic and military assistance is secondary at best. Perhaps the essence of Gorbachev's message to Kim was: Lenin helps those who help themselves.

In short, Gorbachev's immediate priorities appear to be building the internal economy. Some observers argue that Marxism-Leninism, as a binding force externally, has long been dead and useless.[37] Gorbachev's Krasnoyarsk speech in September 1988, which indicated possibilities of initiating trade relations with South Korea and proposed a multilateral discussion on arms reduction on the Korean peninsula, was not as widely reported in Pyongyang as in Seoul. Quite understandably Pyongyang's November 8, 1988, statement conveniently overlooked Gorbachev's Krasnoyarsk proposal. Instead it reiterated the tripartite formula, arguing that "Korea's peace cannot be solved by involving this and that countries in the discussion." For the essence of tension-causing is not from without but from within the Korean peninsula—the North and South Korean and the U.S. military forces.[38]

Given the serious nature of Soviet economic difficulties at home, Gorbachev would have to reduce excessive external subsidies in economic and military assistance. Yet, contrary to Gorbachev's pronouncements, Moscow still continues to provide military assistance for Pyongyang—for example, Mig 23s and SA-3s. It is not known when and with whom these military deliveries had been arranged—in 1984 with Chernenko or with Gorbachev in 1986. On the other hand, even if Moscow would substantially reduce and completely terminate this military assistance, it is not likely to lose an ally in Pyongyang. The peculiar quality of contemporary alliances is that they add very little if anything to the actual might of the Soviet Union other than an illusion of strength.

How has Pyongyang responded thus far? Gorbachev's perestroika could possibly pose a serious dilemma for Pyongyang, whereas it is welcomed in Seoul. Gorbachev's book *Perestroika*, already with three different translations, is selling well in South Korea. It is yet to be available in Pyongyang. Soviet and Chinese reforms could directly challenge the aging North Korean hierarchy. Particularly disturbing to the North Korean leadership must be Gorbachev's calls for greater media openness about Soviet social problems, relaxation of censorship, and demands for more accountability and probity from party officials. While these reforms in the Soviet Union and China have been tenaciously resisted by stubborn party hierarchies,[39] they still could raise a serious doubt in the basic political legitimacy of the North Korean leadership. In the past Khrushchev's de-Stalinization campaign and the subsequent Chinese Cultural Revolution seriously challenged the Pyongyang regime at different times and in different degrees, but now these profound reforms in the two fraternal allies are thrust upon North Korea at the same time.

As in the past, Pyongyang's apprehensive reaction appears to maintain its *chuch'e* (autonomy). This was clearly indicated in the First Session of the 8th Supreme People's Assembly, December 29–30, 1986, when Kim was reelected as the top leader. Kim ordered his country "to guard against the infiltration of the ideological poison of capitalism and revisionism into our society and resolutely struggle against all maneuvers to encroach upon the socialist system."[40] Without any question, the "ideological poison of capitalism and revisionism" refers to the radical reforms in both the Soviet Union and China. Interestingly enough, the title of his 76-minute televised speech was "For the Complete Victory of Socialism." This appears to be somewhat in the opposite direction, at least in public rhetoric, from that of Gorbachev and Deng Xiaoping.[41] Pyongyang's Herculean task is how to improve relations with Moscow and Beijing without being influenced by them internally. Pyongyang's dilemma becomes even more serious when examined in the context of the widening gap in the economic race with Seoul regime.[42]

After more than a year of diplomatic setbacks, by early 1989 Pyongyang slowly seems to be accepting the fact that its socialist friends are ignoring its displeasures and seeking ties with South Korea. This realization has brought a measure of tolerance to North Korean diplomacy. Rather than threatening to sever relations as Pyongyang did with Hungary after it opened an embassy in Seoul, similar pursuit of Seoul by other socialist countries has gone officially unnoticed. Constrained by its policy of self-reliance and cold war ideology, Pyongyang is unlikely to make much headway against the moves toward Seoul. North Korea, though, continues to survive the ideological gap with the more reform-minded Soviets (and Chinese) because of its strategic importance to them.[43]

Gradually but steadily South Korea is moving away from a mendicant diplomacy toward a maturing partnership with the United States. As South Korea comes of age politically and economically, its ties with the United States need basic changes. Both sides' old habits would have to be replaced by new ones, reflecting the new realities.

Offended by the misbehavior of American athletes and press during the Olympics, South Koreans appear to be resenting what they perceive as American bullying of a weaker ally over trade issues. South Korea's sense of pride and independence has grown. More than ever, Seoul finds it dependence on U.S. military support painful, even shameful. While the country has grown economically, the existing U.S.-dominated joint military command structure still reflects the Korean War conditions of the 1950s. Considering the rising tide of Korean nationalism, whether and how long the existing Seoul-Washington relations will last become increasingly questionable.

Reduction of U.S. forces from the Korean peninsula has been openly discussed between Seoul and Washington. The subject of troop reduction is no longer taboo as it once was. Former President Jimmy Carter's unilateral consideration to pull out forces in 1977 was reversed in the face of strong opposition on both sides of the Pacific. But circumstances are quite different now. The South's economy is about five times larger than the North's. Its weapons, perhaps fewer, are considered more advanced. Just as important, ordinary South Koreans now believe they will be able to protect themselves and want to handle their own defense. Similarly, increasing numbers of Americans and their representatives, irritated by Seoul's $10 billion trade surplus with them in 1987, would like to spend less money protecting South Korea, although Seoul allocates 6 percent of its GNP for defense, far more than most U.S. allies.

Military observers in Seoul and Washington recognize the necessity to change their joint command force structure. The majority of the combined forces' troops are Korean, while the commander is American, a fact many Koreans no longer welcome. The United States is also eager to modify the structure so it would not be responsible for misbehavior by the Korean military. Many Koreans, rightly or wrongly, hold the United States responsible for the brutal suppression of the Kwanju uprising in 1980.

Increasing Korean resentment has been targeted lately at the U.S. Yongsan military garrison, a 669-acre base, whose golf course, housing, and headquarters occupy some of Seoul's most expensive downtown real estate—a site equivalent to New York City's Central Park. Reportedly Seoul and Washington have agreed in principle to move the U.S. armed forces headquarters from Yongsan presumably to Daejon. Not only will this relieve Seoul's ever-worsening traffic congestion, but, more importantly, Washington is now highly sensitive toward increasing Korean nationalism. Yongsan, the former headquarters for the Japanese military garrison, has been a symbol of Japanese colonialism. Even this minor adjustment contains potential seeds for trouble between Seoul and Washington. For instance, who will pay for the moving? Given Washington's budget deficit, the new Bush administration will be very reluctant to pay for it. On the other hand, the Roh government, while capable and willing to take care of the moving expenses, will be vehemently opposed not only by radical students but by opposition political parties. Of course, an ideal solution will be sharing the expenses evenly.

Moreover, an antinuclear movement may be gaining steam for the first time in Korea. Many Koreans, for instance, applauded a call for removal of U.S. nuclear weapons by retired U.S. General John Cushman that was broadcast by South Korean government-run TV. This was the first time many Koreans publicly heard of the nuclear weapons' existence. Seoul and Washington have refused to confirm or deny their presence. The retired American general argued that nuclear weapons serve only to fuel anti-American sentiment that could undermine the Seoul-Washington alliance and their removal would preempt demands by students and opposition political parties.[44] Unless and until mutually satisfactory solutions are found to these and other related questions, the widening gap between Seoul and Washington becomes unavoidable as the ties become more mature.

To tackle these and related problems, Seoul has taken bold diplomatic initiatives. Encouraged by the most successful Olympic Games in 12 years, the Roh government has extended economic and political olive branches toward Moscow, Beijing, Pyongyang, and other socialist states. Responding positively, as we noted above, to Gorbachev's Krasnoyarsk proposal, in his major foreign policy address to the UN General Assembly, Roh called for a six-nation "consultative conference for peace" to end the armed standoff between North and South Korea.[45] For the first time, the South Korean president responded positively to Pyongyang's repeated proposal to sign a declaration of nonaggression between the two Koreas. Roh's daring efforts to ease the tension with Pyongyang, largely in response to increasing demand by students and opposition political parties, could eventually lead to a reduction of U.S. forces in Korea.

Judging by Washington's subsequent reactions, Roh's bold UN initiatives had not been fully discussed in advance with the United States. While the general tone of Roh's conciliatory steps to hasten a "springtime for peace and reconciliation on the Korean peninsula" was applauded by Washington,[46] his specific proposal for a six-nation conference apparently surprised the policy makers of the Reagan administration. In fact, Washington observers suspected that the Reagan administration officials would not actively support such a conference—a conference originally proposed by Gorbachev in his Krasnoyarsk speech.

Allegedly complaining for not having been consulted in advance, U.S. Assistant Secretary of State for East Asian and Pacific Affairs Gaston Sigur cast serious doubt about such a conference. In a surprising contrast, Roh's proposal was reportedly supported by the Soviet ambassador to the United Nations.[47] Reagan administration officials feared that Gorbachev's Krasnoyark proposal was basically intended to drive a wedge between Washington and its Pacific allies; so they reacted negatively.[48] Instead they stressed the paramount importance of first reducing tension between North and South Korea.

Ironically enough, this U.S. position is somewhat identical with Pyongyang's latest proposal of November 7, 1988.[49] Judging from its content, Pyongyang is not likely to have discussed it in advance with Moscow. Stressing the importance of the tripartite conference—initially proposed by the United States but rejected by the Soviet Union—Pyongyang claims that "the problem of peace cannot be solved by means of creating an 'international environment' by involving this or that country into the discussion of the Korean question, ignoring the root cause of war on the Korean peninsula."[50] In all probability, neither the six-nation conference nor tripartite talks can fundamentally solve the Korean question. Only the two Koreas, and nobody else, can find the lasting national solution.

For such a solution, Roh has repeated his offer for a summit meeting with Kim Il Sung. Expressing his willingness to sign a nonaggression declaration, he pledged also that "the Republic of Korea will never use force first against the North."[51] On the fortieth anniversary of the founding of the government in Pyongyang in September 1988, Kim Il Sung also proposed such top-level talks. This was repeated by Kang Sok Ju, first vice-foreign minister of North Korea, in his UN address on October 19, 1988. The latest Pyongyang communiqué of November 7, 1988, claimed that "the top-level talks will be a weighty event of epochal significance on the road of achieving peace in the country and the cause of peaceful reunification."[52]

Reversing its stand, Seoul also urged its Western allies to improve relations with Pyongyang. Allegedly encouraged by Seoul, Washington has eased, since October 31, 1988, some curbs on North Korea. Travel restrictions between the United States and North Korea have been loosened, a trade ban eased slightly to allow the sale of "humanitarian goods" like food and clothing to the North Koreans, and diplomats representing Washington and Pyongyang have met in neutral settings at least three times.[53] At a private academic level, the International Strategic Institute at Stanford University in California (ISIS) reportedly agreed, early in November 1988, to establish academic exchange between ISIS and the North Korean Academy of Sciences, beginning February 1989. To date, there has been little substantive progress in U.S.-North Korean relations. At their third meeting in February 1989 in Beijing, the United States said that it was premature to hold trilateral talks about the Korean peninsula and that it was more important that North and South should talk to each other first.[54]

Indeed, these are times for profound changes in the geopolitical landscape in Northeast Asia. Yet in perspective, the U.S. defense umbrella has helped set the stage for South Korea's economic miracle. Political development toward democracy and away from harsh military rule has begun under the Roh administration. These remarkable developments should strengthen, not strain, ties between Seoul and Washington. But to do this, perhaps the sooner the big-brother, little-brother relationship terminates the better. A new, mature relationship should take its place. How the new Bush administration will establish such a relationship remains to be seen.

CONCLUSION

One sure way to look into the uncertain future is to look back. Undeniably Gorbachev has been largely responsible for having rejuvenated the urgency of solving the Korean issue through his daring Asian-Pacific initiatives of 1986 and 1988. In order to cope with serious domestic economic problems, the Soviet leadership under Gorbachev has concluded that a favorable international environment is essential. This, in turn, can be established by resolving nagging regional issues, which was clearly indicated at the Soviet-U.S. Moscow summit in June 1988. The rapidly changing external environment surrounding the Korean peninsula and its fluid internal dynamics, particularly in the South, has been remarkably receptive to Gorbachev's initiatives.

For these initiatives to bear fruit, what are the necessary and sufficient ingredients, external and internal? Potential benefits notwithstanding, Gorbachev's initiatives are not likely to be successful with lingering old ties between Moscow and Pyongyang, on the one hand, and between Seoul and Washington, on the other. Yet these ties can be readily modified by either of the two major powers and the two Koreas. Only then may it be possible for the two Koreas to reassociate themselves.

What then could Moscow and Washington do? In full consultation with Pyongyang and Seoul, they could conceivably issue a joint policy statement.[55] They could pledge, for instance, to terminate and to refrain from any further political-military confrontation in the Korean peninsula. Such a joint public statement could function as a major catalyst for a serious interaction between the North and the South to improve their mutual relations. Moscow and Washington may also attempt to transform the existing military truce, since July 1953, into a stable peace. Mindful of the Korean people's fervent desire for their peaceful reunification, the two major powers could solemnly promise to support the reunification of Korea.

In the final analysis, of course, the Koreans themselves must be responsible for achieving their own reunification. Under such circumstances, the North and the South could pledge to no use of force, noninterference in each other's internal affairs, and to stop slandering each other. In order to prevent any accidental conflict, they could conceivably establish direct telephone, fax, and other means of communications.

In all probability, Moscow is not likely to improve relations with Seoul at the expense of its much more important relations with Washington. Also, despite the prevailing Soviet euphoria in Seoul, Seoul cannot possibly afford to replace the huge U.S. market—nearly 35 percent of South Korea's exports—even with combined markets in the Soviet Union and China.

Perhaps even more significant are internal considerations. For no analysis of any state's foreign policy process would be complete without devoting some attention to the role of internal politics. In North Korea there is a more relaxed political mood as the country prepared to welcome the World Youth Festival in July 1989. Pyongyang's determination to turn the festival into a showcase rival to the

1988 Olympics has contributed to a newfound flexibility and accommodation of foreign interests. As well, the regime is also encouraging joint ventures to attract foreign technology and generate export earnings. The changes in mood and policies do not necessarily represent fundamental changes. North Korean officials still assert that their system is perfect and that Soviet and Chinese-style reforms are designed to meet specific conditions in other countries. Analysts caution that as long as Kim Il Sung lives, North Korea is unlikely to undergo more radical change.[56]

The acid test of Gorbachev's initiatives is his ability to obtain domestic support in two areas: the problem of legitimizing a policy within the Soviet governmental apparatus, which is a problem of bureaucratic rationality; and that of harmonizing it with the national experience, which is a problem of historical development.[57] These two conditions are also applicable to South Korea. To forge a successful *buk-bang oae-kyo*, the Roh government has to establish a multipartisanship based on a systematically coordinated foreign policy between academics, business, and government.

Indeed, these are historic challenges. While Gorbachev and Roh have been successful thus far beyond expectations and reforms in North Korea remain tentative, all of these nations have just begun their long journey into the exciting twenty-first Pacific century.

NOTES

1. The complete text of the speech is found in *Pravda*, July 29, 1986 as translated in *Daily Report-Soviet Union* (Foreign Broadcast Information Service, hereafter FBIS), July 29, 1986, pp. R1-20.

2. Professor Seweryn Bialer suggests six major sources: the crisis of the Soviet system under Brezhnev, the economy, the changed nature of the Soviet society, the technological change in the West, the deteriorated Soviet international position, and the ascent of an entire new generation to leadership. For details see Bialer, "Gorbachev's Program of Change: Sources, Significance, Prospects," *Political Science Quarterly* 103 (Fall 1988): 403-460.

3. The complete text of the interview is found in *Time*, September 9, 1985, pp. 22-28.

4. Mikhail Gorbachev, *Perestroika: New Thinking for Our Country and the World* (New York: Harper and Row, 1987), p. 17.

5. A prominent Soviet historian, Yuri N. Afanaseyev, edited a volume, *Inogo ne dano* (*No Other Alternatives*) (Moscow: Progress, 1988), containing 34 essays

by well-known public figures. Apparently this is a rather popular book in the Soviet Union, available recently only in hard-currency book stores.

6. Abel Aganbegyan, *The Challenge: Economics of Perestroika* (London: Hutchinson, 1988), p. 1.

7. Ed A. Hewett, *Reforming the Soviet Economy: Equality versus Efficiency* (Washington, D.C.: The Brookings Institution, 1988), p. 306.

8. Much has been written about economic difficulties in the Soviet Far East: Paval Minakir, "Perestroika in the Soviet Economy and the Economic Development of the Far East," a lecture at Harvard University, May 31, 1988; Hiroshi Kimura, "Soviet Focus on the Pacific," *Problems of Communism* 36 (May–June 1987): 1-15; Gerald Segal, "The USSR and Asia in 1987: Signs of a Major Effort," *Asian Survey* 28, no. 1 (January 1988): 1-9.

9. *The Economist*, August 20, 1988, p. 16.

10. Young-kee Kown, "Crisis Theory After the Olympics," *Wolgan-Chosen*, August 1988, pp. 132-145; this essay is based on 30 elite opinion polls in Korea.

11. *The Economist*, May 21, 1988, p. 4.

12. *Wall Street Journal*, November 4, 1988, p. A12.

13. *The Korean Political Tradition and Law: Essays in Korean Law and Legal History* (Seoul: Royal Asiatic Society, Korea Branch, Hollyn Corporation: 1971), p. 21.

14. Soviet Japan specialists seem well aware that Tokyo intends on making possible Japanese economic cooperation with Moscow a hostage to the Northern Territories issue. They do not necessarily agree with Japanese Soviet experts that the Soviet Union will have to give up the Northern Territories because without Japan's economic assistance, the long-term Soviet Far Eastern development plan (calling for investment of 200 billion rubles, or 40 trillion yen by the year 2000) will be in jeopardy. For a detailed study, see Roy Kim, *Soviet-Japanese Relations Under Gorbachev* (Pittsburgh: Russian and East European Study Center, University of Pittsburgh, 1988); a somewhat optimistic view is expressed by Gerald Segal, "Moscow Adopts a New Realistic Line on Japan," *Far Eastern Economic Review*, October 6, 1988, pp. 79-80; still another view, "that Japan does not rank highly in Soviet literature or media comment," is expressed by Myles L. C. Robertson, *Soviet Policy Towards Japan: An Analysis of Trends in the 1970s and 1980s* (Cambridge: Cambridge University Press, 1988), p. 185.

15. Detailed information, including a 13-article constitution and the composition of the committee, is found in "The Soviet Union in Asia-Pacific Region: Economic Development and Cooperation." *SOVNAPEC Newsletter*, May 1988. I am grateful to academician Yevgeni Primakov for providing me this information.

16. As an observer designated by Dr. Mark Borthwick, executive director of the U.S. National Committee for Pacific Economic Cooperation, I attended the Osaka gathering and held discussions with Soviet representatives Yevgeni Primakov and Drs. Vladimir Lukin and Vladimir Ibanov.

17. Ralph N. Clough, *Embattled Korea* (Boulder, CO: Westview Press, 1987), p. 334.
18. Ibid.
19. *New York Times*, February 5, 1988, p. 3.
20. "South Korea Is Warming Up to China and Russia," *Business Week*, April 18, 1988, p. 43.
21. Daewoo's CEO Kim Woo-jong's interview, *Dong-A Ilbo*, April 13, 1988.
22. *Korea Newsreview*, October 11, 1988, p. 11.
23. The entire speech from *Pravda* can be found in *Daily Report-Soviet Union* (FBIS), September 20, 1988, pp. 29-41.
24. *The Economist*, September 24, 1988, p. 38.
25. *Beijing Review*, October 16, 1988, p. 14; a conservative *Japan Economic Journal* editorial, "Siberian Thaw?" appeared on October 1, 1988.
26. *New Times*, October 1, 1988.
27. Address by His Excellency Mr. Roh Tae Woo, President of the Republic of Korea, at the 43rd Session of the General Assembly of the United Nations, October 18, 1988, New York, p. 9.
28. *Asian Wall Street Journal*, October 17, 1988.
29. *Pravda*, February 17, 1987 in *Daily Report-Soviet Union* (FBIS), February 17, 1987, p. A12.
30. *USSR-USA: Summit, Moscow, May 29-June 2, 1988, Documents and Materials* (Moscow: Novosti Press Agency Publishing House, 1988), p. 89.
31. Ibid.
32. A statement is quoted in *Dong-A Ilbo*, November 7, 1988.
33. *Pravda*, October 26, 1986 in *Daily Report-Soviet Union* (FBIS), October 28, 1986, p. C4.
34. Ibid., p. C5.
35. The complete text is found in *Moscow News*, July 10-17, 1988, *supplement*, pp. 1-13.
36. An excellent analysis of Gorbachev's overall relations with the Third World is provided by Francis Fukuyama, "Gorbachev and the Third World," *Foreign Affairs*, Spring 1986, pp. 715-731.
37. Vladimir Petrov, "Gorbachev Looks at Asia," *Journal of Northeast Asian Studies* 4 (Winter 1985): 32.
38. *Korean Central News Agency*, November 8, 1988.
39. Two such notable figures reportedly have been Dinmukhamed Kunayev and Vladimir Shcherbitsky, the party chiefs of Kazakhstan and Ukraine. Kunayev's ouster in December 1986 was followed by unprecedented large riots in Alma-Ata, the capital of Kazakhstan. Kunayev, originally appointed by Leonid Brezhenev, went to Pyongyang in January 1978 to present Kim Il Sung with an Order of Lenin that had been awarded by the Supreme Soviet in 1972. Ralph N. Clough, "The Soviet Union and the Two Koreas," *Soviet Policy in East Asia*, ed. Donald A. Zagoria (New Haven, CT: Yale University Press, 1982), p. 182.

40. The complete speech is found in *Rodong Shinmun*, December 31, 1986.

41. "Let Russia Join the Dance," *The Economist*, January 3-9, 1987, pp. 9-10.

42. Seoul's 1986 per capita gross national product was reported to have reached $2,270 while Pyongyang stagnated at less than $800; see *Wall Street Journal*, January 15, 1987, pp. 1, 5.

43. "Reality Presses In," *Far Eastern Economic Review*, April 27, 1989, p. 32.

44. Ibid.

45. Roh's UN address.

46. This was expressed after the Reagan-Roh summit on October 20 in Washington. *Washington Post*, October 21, 1988.

47. This was clearly indicated in his briefing on the Reagan-Roh summit. For the complete text see *Dong-A Ilbo*, October 24, 1988.

48. For specifics, see Gaston J. Sigur and Richard Armitage, "To Play in Asia, Moscow Has to Pay," *New York Times*, October 2, 1988.

49. *Korean Central News Agency*, November 8, 1988.

50. Ibid.

51. Roh's UN address.

52. *Korean Central News Agency*, November 8, 1988.

53. Robert Delfs, "Delicate Dialogue," *Far Eastern Economic Review*, February 9, 1989, pp. 18-19.

54. "Reality Presses In," p. 32.

55. Regarding this matter, I have benefited from a joint publication by the International Strategic Institute at Stanford University and the Institute of Far Eastern Studies, Academy of Sciences of the USSR, *On Strengthening Security and Developing Cooperation on the Korean Peninsula, a Special Report of the Center for International Security and Arms Control* (Stanford, CA: Stanford University, 1988).

56. Louise do Rosario, "Iron Fist Relaxes," *Far Eastern Economic Review*, April 27, 1988, pp. 32-33; Urban C. Lehner, "North Koreans Hide Poverty Behind Showcase Projects," *Wall Street Journal*, July 11, 1989, p. A14.

57. Henry Kissinger, *A World Restored* (Boston: Houghton Mifflin, 1957), p. 326.

CHAPTER 7

Conclusion: Assessing the Impact of Glasnost and Perestroika

CHARLES BUKOWSKI

While there seems to be little question that Gorbachev's reforms have had an impact on many other socialist states, the direction and extent of that impact is very much open to question. As David Mason explained in Chapter 1, glasnost and perestroika involve a number of foreign and domestic policy undertakings affecting many aspects of the Soviet economic, political, and social systems. Just as glasnost and perestroika are having a widespread impact within the Soviet Union, they also carry the potential to influence other socialist states in a diverse manner. Understanding and systematizing this influence will be a complex task—a task made no less easy by the tremendous diversity that exists within the socialist community.

At this time, it is beyond our capability to determine specific policies of socialist states that might arise as a result of glasnost and perestroika. Gorbachev's reforms have been in effect for too short a time and (more importantly) our understanding of the policy-making process of socialist systems is sadly inadequate. No doubt glasnost and perestroika are just one set of factors that might affect the policy-making process of socialist states. This is a complex task and suggests that the problem be approached in as systematic a manner as possible. One method that may be useful is the construction of a framework or model that is representative of the policy-making function of socialist systems and is capable of incorporating the impact of external phenomena such as the recent Soviet reforms.

The remainder of this chapter will present a simple model of the policy-making process for socialist countries and use that model to examine how the Soviet policies of glasnost and perestroika might affect the policy-making process of the countries examined in this volume. It should be noted that the primary purpose of this model is not to enhance our understanding of policy making in socialist systems, but to permit the comparative analysis of the countries discussed in this volume in as orderly and consistent a manner as possible. The policy-making model will suggest several categories of variables that will be analyzed on a cross-national basis. Such an analysis will permit a more systematic study of the role glasnost and perestroika play in the rest of the socialist community. It then should be possible to make preliminary determinations about the different ways in which the countries under study in this volume might be reacting to the recent Soviet reforms.

The contents of the previous chapters suggest that glasnost and perestroika may affect the socialist community in a variety of ways. In terms of policy, their impact will be apparent in both the domestic and foreign policy-making process. Any model that attempts to analyze such an impact must include provisions for both categories of policy. This should not be surprising. Kuhlman has argued that "increasingly, national actors tend to view domestic and foreign policy decision-making in the same overall framework."[1] He suggests that a useful way of characterizing policy making in a political system is in terms of a single public policy-making process.

The public policy-making approach suggested by Kuhlman reflects an earlier contention by Hilsman and others[2] that the line between foreign and domestic policy is becoming increasingly blurred as more issues that used to have only domestic significance now have certain foreign policy implications and vice versa. As a result, it makes sense to build a model that conceives of all government policy as the result of a combination of the same broad range of variables. The intensity of the impact of variables will differ from one type of issue to another, but the ultimate range and variety of variables will remain constant regardless of whether the policy is viewed as foreign or domestic.

This work will adopt a model constructed by Kuhlman,[3] which will be greatly simplified for use here since it is intended only as a means of systematically examining the data presented in the previous chapters, rather than as a tool for understanding the policy-making processes of states. Kuhlman's model emphasizes the need to recognize the role played in the policy process by various domestic factors, and that this role can be understood best by examining the impact of factors on a cross-national basis. He selects four groups of factors that he finds relevant to the policy process: historical-cultural, social-economic, organizational-institutional, and elite-factions. In general, the degree of impact these factors may have on policy conversion will increase in ascending order, with elite-factions being the most important group. Kuhlman is careful to caution that he does not mean to overemphasize the role played by domestic factors in the public policy process. Rather he contends that the role these factors play deserve greater and more systematic, cross-national investigation than they have received in the past.

Policy outputs are viewed as the result of policy conversion, which is activated by a range of "policy-relevant" issues, both foreign and domestic in origin. Actual policy conversion will be conditioned by Kuhlman's four factor categories. Thus public policy, in all its manifestations, can be investigated using a single approach and by focusing on the same categories of factors. At the obvious risk of overlooking certain idiosyncracies in each system, it becomes possible to compare, cross-nationally, the policy process of various political systems and to attempt to arrive at tentative generalizations about those systems.

The utility of the proposed model in determining the impact of glasnost and perestroika on the socialist community is twofold. First, it suggests a list of factor categories to be examined for each country that might, in some way, be susceptible to the consequences of the Soviet reforms. Second, it allows specific (or policy-relevant) issues raised by the Soviet Union to be inserted into the policy conversion step of the policy-making process. By applying this model on a cross-national basis, similar questions will be posed for each country under study in this volume. While the answers are certain to vary from country to country, the consistency of the questions should assist in the search for generalizations about the impact of glasnost and perestroika. For example, some countries may be more susceptible to the impact of the Soviet reforms because of certain historical or cultural attributes, while for others the impact may be minimal. In addition, glasnost and perestroika may raise an important issue for one political system, while for another it may not be an issue at all.

EXAMINATION OF FACTOR CATEGORIES

The analysis presented in this section does not pretend to be a comprehensive study of the impact of glasnost and perestroika. Instead, it represents an attempt to summarize the data presented in the previous chapters in a cross-national manner with the hope that tentative conclusions can be drawn about what Gorbachev's new policies will mean for other socialist systems.

Historical-Cultural

Two important items that can be included in the historical-cultural category are the character and length of a country's relationship with the Soviet Union. For example, Mason (Chapter 1) suggests that a key change in the Soviet relationship with its East European allies is that the Kremlin is no longer allied with opponents of reform. Rather than acting as a brake on the reform process in Eastern Europe, the Soviets are now offering encouragement.

Given the duration and closeness of the relationship between the Soviet Union and its East European allies, it is likely that the impact of glasnost and perestroika will be felt sooner and more strongly in Eastern Europe than elsewhere in the socialist community. (In this regard, China's proximity to the Soviet Union also must be considered. In Chapter 2 Walsh indicates that the student demonstrations in China in the spring of 1989 were partially inspired by Soviet political reforms.) In addition, the East European states have a more important role in Gorbachev's reform plans than other socialist states. Mason notes that some of the success of perestroika will depend on Eastern Europe's ability to supply the Soviet economy with technologically sophisticated products. At the very least, the Soviets hope that Eastern Europe will no longer be an economic burden to them.

Another important role Mason and others have suggested for Eastern Europe is that of a testing ground. Many of Gorbachev's reforms are already being tried in various East European countries. Given the relative similarities of the Soviet and East European systems, the Soviets can learn from the experiences of their neighbors and perhaps lessen the risks of reform.

Walsh shows that the Soviets also hope to learn something from the Chinese economic reforms. Conversely, the Soviets have suggested that the Chinese can learn from the Soviet policy of glasnost.

Certainly Gorbachev's support of the student demonstrators in China in 1989 reflects this idea.

Recent historical and cultural factors associated with Poland and Czechoslovakia may help determine how Gorbachev's programs will be received. Among all of the Soviet Union's East European allies, Poland probably has been the least accepting of Soviet-type socialism. Reforms that would encourage economic decentralization and political openness would be compatible with socialist Poland's political culture.

In the case of Czechoslovakia, Mason writes of the dilemma of reform facing the leadership. With many of Gorbachev's reforms resembling those of the Dubcek era, the current leadership must take care not to undermine its own legitimacy. The Soviets and the Czechoslovaks also must come to terms with the Brezhnev Doctrine. Explicit repudiation of the Brezhnev Doctrine also could have a negative impact on the legitimacy of the Czechoslovak regime, with related consequences for the entire region.

Cuba's relationship with the Soviet Union soon will be entering its fourth decade. Yet despite this longevity, del Aguila (Chapter 3) illustrates that the Cuban political system faces a much different set of historical and cultural circumstances than Poland or Czechoslovakia. Castro continues to portray his regime as revolutionary and centralized in nature (del Aguila writes that Castro may be the last true believer). Castro's aggressive foreign and domestic policies reflect this. Gorbachev's reforms call into question not only the centralized structure of the Cuban regime, but also its lack of tolerance for domestic dissent. Castro also must deal with the continued presence and threat of the United States. It is not surprising that del Aguila sees little prospect for interest in glasnost and perestroika in Cuba. Castro has repeatedly rejected the utility of such reforms for Cuba, and he showed no sign of changing his mind during his April 1989 summit with Gorbachev. For the historical-cultural factor category, Cuba presents itself as a system that is very unresponsive to the idea of reform.

In contrast to Cuba, recent historical and cultural factors relating to Vietnam suggest that glasnost and perestroika have had an impact on the Vietnamese policy process. In fact, Papp (Chapter 4) notes that the Vietnamese leadership discussed the need for serious reform before Gorbachev came to power. Papp also points out that, like Gorbachev, the Vietnamese leadership has had difficulty implementing reform. The new generation of leaders in Vietnam appears less interested in characterizing itself as revolutionary. Rather, it is receptive to change and cognizant of the lack of progress Vietnam has made since its unification.

North Korea and Afghanistan represent two more cases in which historical and cultural factors are likely to hinder the effects of glasnost and perestroika. The North Korean case is, in some ways, similar to the Cuban situation (Kim, Chapter 6). The original revolutionary leadership continues to survive, and to legitimate its rule on past accomplishments. Acknowledgment of the need for reform would undermine the authenticity of past undertakings and the reputation of the regime.

The Afghan socialist leadership faces a more desperate situation. Blank (Chapter 5) notes that support for the Kabul government is very narrow in Afghanistan. It had little, if any, legitimacy in the first place. Yet with several active and powerful rebel movements representing alternatives to the socialist regime, the Kabul government has little room for maneuvering. In addition, the severity of the crisis facing the government makes discussion of reform unfeasible. Nor does it appear that the leadership has ever been receptive to the idea of reform in the past.

In the case of China, Walsh shows that the Chinese themselves have argued that China is not developed enough, politically or culturally, to undertake a program resembling glasnost. However, Chinese society, for historical and cultural reasons, is more receptive to economic reform than Soviet society, and, in most cases, Chinese economic reform has gone much farther than Soviet efforts. In fact, as noted earlier, the Soviets have indicated that they can learn a great deal from the Chinese experiments.

The issue of general receptiveness to reform also can be applied to all the systems in question in a more general way. Knowledge of a particular system's political culture, both past and present, can assist in the building of a better understanding of how glasnost and perestroika might be received. For example, Czechoslovakia, historically, has been receptive to change while Afghanistan has not.

Social-Economic

The social-economic factor category suggests a number of areas in which glasnost and perestroika might affect a nation's public policy output. One must examine the nature of a system's economic ties with the Soviet Union. Papp notes that the Vietnamese leadership is very aware of its high degree of dependence on the Soviet Union for economic and military aid as well as trade. While such a situation does not guarantee compliance (as Kim and del Aguila point out for North Korea and Cuba, respectively), it must certainly play a role in the policy process. A more germane question with regard to this issue is determining whether and to what extent the Soviets are willing to use this lever to encourage reform elsewhere. (This issue will be addressed subsequently in the discussion of the policy conversion portion of the model.)

The Chinese case is unique. Beijing embarked on a program of economic reform before Gorbachev assumed power. Yet China's poor economic performance under the revolutionary regime was a key factor in the decision to undertake sweeping economic reforms.

A second variable suggested by this category is the current conditions of a country's social and economic structures. The dismal state of the Polish economy and high degree of unrest that exists in Polish society no doubt were important factors in the leadership's decision to recognize Solidarity and democratize the Polish political process. Similarly, Papp notes the sad condition of the Vietnamese economy.

Cuba and North Korea also are facing problems of lack of economic performance, but show little interest in reform. The public policy-making model utilized here understands policy as the result of a complex interaction of variables. Thus, while economic or social instability can contribute to a particular policy decision, they are by no means sole contributors. Rather, one must look at all factor categories in order to understand why a policy choice has been made.

Organizational-Institutional

Kuhlman uses the dual category designation of organizational-institutional to distinguish between organizations that are officially a part of the policy process (such as the Communist Party) and institutions that may not be sanctioned but nevertheless play a part in determining policy (such as dissident groups or churches). Kuhlman also includes the constitutional structure of a country in this factor category. In the case of this volume, attention must be directed at the federal structure of Czechoslovakia's constitution, the 1989 constitutional changes in Poland, and the tenuous nature of the socialist government in Afghanistan.

Perhaps the most important item to consider in this category is the condition and orientation of the Communist Party of each state. (This factor will be closely linked to the orientation of the party leadership, which will be examined in the elite-factions factor category.) Yet it may be useful to attempt to arrive at some conclusions regarding overall party character. For example, the Polish United Workers' Party has presided over numerous changes in Poland's political, economic, and social systems. The Vietnamese Communist Party (CPV) also has had a turbulent history. While formal reforms in the Vietnamese system have not been numerous, the pragmatic nature of the party is evident in its success in fighting French, U.S., and Chinese invaders. It should not be surprising that the CPV discussed the need for significant economic reform in Vietnam before Gorbachev adopted his reform program. In contrast, the Communist parties of North Korea and Cuba traditionally have shown little interest in reform.

Another important part of the organizational-institutional category is the state of unofficial interest groups in a particular socialist system. Most of these groups would be likely to favor political, economic, or social reforms. Among the countries under consideration in this volume, certainly Poland possesses the greatest number as well as the most influential of the unofficial interest groups. Mason notes that Solidarity and other opposition groups had become so influential that the government found it had no other choice but to seek their cooperation. The end result of the long-running standoff between the government and the opposition is the historic agreement of April 1989, which opened up the political process to noncommunist groups. A somewhat similar process is occurring in Hungary. Mason also describes in his chapter a growing opposition in Czechoslovakia. While lacking in influence, these opposition groups are becoming increasingly vocal and could provide a source of support for a reform-minded individual within the party ranks.

The other countries examined in this volume do not possess unofficial interest groups to the same extent as the East European states. Yet such groups do exist. Del Aguila notes several groups in Cuba that are likely to be supportive of glasnost and perestroika. Papp suggests a similar state of affairs exists in Vietnam. The situation in North Korea is less clear. In Afghanistan, the government is able to remain intact only with massive Soviet assistance. However, the groups opposing the government are armed rebels, and there is no reason to believe they will accept any form of communism.

Unofficial interest groups can best be thought of as an indicator of potential receptiveness to glasnost and perestroika. They represent an opportunity and provide potential resources for those within the leadership, or are aspiring to leadership, who might be reform minded.

Elite-Factions

As with the preceding factor category, elites are understood to include important individuals regardless of whether their status is official or unofficial. In addition, factions, whether part of the party or part of unofficial interest groups, "can be significant influences of outcomes, either as factions that form around specific identities or as issue-oriented factions."[4]

Kuhlman considers this category as having the greatest overall impact on the policy-making process. Individuals are commonly viewed as having ultimate responsibility for making policy. This is no less the case in the study of socialist systems where a great deal of work has focused on communist elites.[5]

No doubt the most important element in this category will be the receptiveness of key elites to reform. In this case, the content of the previous chapters does little to overturn conventional wisdom, and so there is no need to examine the conclusions of the contributors in great detail. Countries that have leaders that support Gorbachev's reforms are obviously more likely to incorporate similar ideas in their policy-making processes. This propensity will be reinforced or undermined by the content of the previous factor categories.

Mason suggests that a good indicator of receptiveness to reform is age. Elites that have been in power for a relatively short period of time are more likely to encourage reform. Communist leaders whose tenures exceed ten years are in a precarious position with respect to meaningful reform. Effective justification of a reform program requires that past policies be viewed as failures. In short, a leader would have to criticize his own previous policies and thus call into question his right to lead. Other items in this factor category that warrant consideration include unofficial elites (religious figures, noted dissidents, etc.) and official and unofficial factions, as suggested by Kuhlman.

Glasnost, Perestroika, and the Policy-Making Process

Thus far this chapter has examined how various domestic factors that shape the policy-making process might be affected by glasnost and perestroika. It is also important to understand how the Soviet Union might seek to directly influence policy outcomes in other socialist countries. With respect to the model used here, Soviet influence (along with other external factors) can be viewed as impacting on policy conversion.

While Soviet influence can be rather easily incorporated into the model, it is much more difficult to establish that influence in reality. All of the contributors to this volume have indicated that the Soviets would find it beneficial if other socialist states adopted reforms similar to Gorbachev's. Most of the contributors have suggested areas in which the nations under investigation would be vulnerable to Soviet pressure. Yet there is little solid evidence to prove that the Soviets actually have tried to force reforms on other socialist countries. For example, Papp notes that it would be reasonable to assume that the Soviets have encouraged reform in Vietnam, but, as yet, there is no firm evidence of such an occurrence.

Mason writes that the Soviet approach seems to be a positive one. Gorbachev understands the difficulties and risks of forcing a policy on another country. His approach is one of providing positive incentives (and verbal encouragement) to those countries that are willing to undertake reform. For those countries that are not inclined toward glasnost and perestroika, sanctions are not likley, but these countries are unlikely to receive additional benefits from Moscow. This appears to be the case with Cuba. Del Aguila concludes that there is no reason to believe that the Soviets are trying to force reforms on Castro, nor do the Soviets show any signs of reducing their aid to Cuba.

Gorbachev is well aware of the risks and consequences of reform. He has experienced many of those consequences himself. By encouraging reform in other socialist countries, he places them at risk as well. For Gorbachev, the most prudent approach toward the socialist community would be to limit the risks to those leaderships that will undertake reform voluntarily. Glasnost and perestroika can easily fail under the guidance of an enthusiastic leadership. Under an unwilling leader, reform would have little chance of success. The best formula for future progress is a record of past success. Gorbachev needs his initial reforms to succeed, both within the USSR and in other socialist countries, if he wishes to pursue reform in the long run. Forcing reforms on unwilling leaders would jeopardize the chances for initial success. For the time being, it is unlikely that the Soviets will attempt to do anything more than simply encourage other socialist states to undertake reforms.

There is one additional aspect of the model that deserves attention: the impact of changes in the issues processed by the model. This aspect is reflected in the contention by some of the contributors that the impact of glasnost and perestroika will vary according to issue area. For example, Papp notes that the Vietnamese policy process will be most affected by glasnost and perestroika when it deals with foreign and national security issues. Afghanistan's heavy dependence on the Soviet Union for military aid suggests a similar situation.

The range of issues affected by glasnost and perestroika among the East European countries is likely to be broader given the more extensive relations that exist between the Soviet Union and that region. Certainly this is the case in Poland. Mason describes similarities between Gorbachev's reforms and Jaruzelski's attempts at reconciliation with the opposition. In this case, the relationship appears to go both ways, with Moscow expressing as much interest in what is happening in Poland as the Polish leadership does for Soviet efforts.

CONCLUSION

The contributors to this volume present a number of very different conclusions regarding the impact of glasnost and perestroika on the socialist community. Yet they all show that Gorbachev and his reforms in the Soviet Union have had, and will continue to have, significant implications for every socialist country. In some cases, most notably Poland, glasnost and perestroika are being welcomed and used to encourage reform. In other cases, such as Czechoslovakia, the leadership is only reluctantly taking measures to imitate Soviet actions. In still other cases, such as Cuba and North Korea, while glasnost and perestroika are rejected as inappropriate, these leaderships are still forced to come to terms with the issue of reform.

As noted above, the nations of the socialist community have made selective use of glasnost and perestroika. The review of the four factor categories illustrates how various system characteristics can influence the manner in which a country is affected by, or responds to, the Soviet reforms. In Poland, glasnost and perestroika have influenced virtually every aspect of public policy. The Chinese have tried to confine reform to the economic sector, but find that they must also address the issue of political reform. The Vietnamese are experimenting with economic reform as well and have tried, with limited success, to limit the effects of Soviet reform on their foreign and defense policies.

Perhaps the most important question is where will the reform process lead, both for the Soviet Union and throughout the socialist community? This question can only be answered fully with the passage of time. Yet, as the reform process continues, greater scrutiny must be given to its implications and consequences for both the USSR and the other socialist states. First, there must continue to be an awareness that glasnost and perestroika carry significant risks as well as benefits to those countries that pursue reform. Second, the Soviets must be prepared to deal with the adverse consequences of their own reforms as well as those of their allies. The Soviets have encouraged reform in Poland and must deal with the consequences should the Polish government lose control of the situation. Gorbachev's own reputation may suffer as a result of the mistakes of others outside the USSR. Thus a major factor affecting the future of the Soviet reform effort lies outside Gorbachev's control. Third, the initiatives of other socialist states may give momentum to the reform process in the Soviet Union. Should the Polish experiments be successful, Gorbachev can pursue his own agenda with more confidence. Relatedly, reforms in other socialist countries may push the Soviet reform process faster than Gorbachev is willing to go. Fourth, Gorbachev may decide to more actively pursue change in other socialist countries. Thus far, as has been discussed, the evidence suggests that Gorbachev has done little to persuade countries such as Cuba or North Korea to undertake their own versions of glasnost and perestroika. Gorbachev could decide to exert greater pressure on Castro or Kim in the future (or on their successors). Similar options exist for Gorbachev in Eastern Europe.

Regardless of what the future brings for the Soviet Union and the rest of the socialist community, it is clear that the nature of socialism in the world has been profoundly changed by Mikhail Gorbachev. Every socialist country in the world has had to come to terms with glasnost and perestroika, whether it wished to or not. Similarly, scholars in the field of comparative socialist studies must come to terms with glasnost and perestroika. While scholars may arrive at conflicting conclusions about what Gorbachev's reforms mean and whether they will be successful, it is important that they study these changes in a systematic fashion. It would be unrealistic to expect every scholar to arrive at similar answers, but, for the discipline to benefit, they must at least ask the same questions.

NOTES

1. James A. Kuhlman, "A Framework for Viewing Domestic and Foreign Policy Patterns," in *The International Politics of Eastern Europe*, ed. Charles Gati (New York: Praeger Publishers, 1976), p. 275.

2. See Roger Hilsman, "The Foreign-Policy Consensus: An Interim Research Report," *Journal of Conflict Resolution*, December 1959: 361-382; and Charles W. Kegley, Jr. and Eugene R. Wittkopf, *American Foreign Policy: Pattern and Process*, 3rd ed. (New York: St. Martin's Press, 1987), pp. 247-250.

3. Kuhlman, "A Framework," pp. 275-291.

4. Ibid., p. 280.

5. For example, see Carl Beck et al., *Comparative Communist Political Leadership* (New York: David McKay, 1973); Valerie Bunce, *Do New Leaders Make a Difference? Executive Succession and Public Policy Under Capitalism and Socialism* (Princeton, NJ: Princeton University Press, 1981); and Martin McCauley and Stephen Carter, eds., *Leadership and Succession in the Soviet Union, Eastern Europe and China* (Armonk, NY: M. E. Sharpe, 1986).

Selected Bibliography

Aganbeygan, Abel. *The Challenge: Economics of Perestroika.* London: Hutchinson, 1988.
Almqvist, B. "The Afghan War in 1983: Strengthened Resistance Versus 'Nazi Tactics'." *Central Asian Survey* 4 (1984): 23-46.
Amin, A. Rasul. "A General Reflection on the Stealthy Sovietization of Afghanistan." *Central Asian Survey* 3, no. 1 (1984): 58-61.
Amin, A. Rasul, and Nazeem Rizvi. "Sovietization of Afghanistan." *Strategic Studies* (Islamabad) 11 (Summer 1988).
Amstutz, J. Bruce. *Afghanistan: The First Five Years of Soviet Occupation.* Washington, D.C.: National Defense University Press, 1986.
Anwar, Raja. *The Tragedy of Afghanistan: A First-Hand Account.* London: Verso Books, 1988.
Arnold, Ruth, and Anthony Arnold. "Afghanistan." In *Yearbook on International Communist Affairs, 1988*, edited by Richard F. Staar. Stanford, CA: Hoover Institution Press, 1988.
——— . *Afghanistan's Two Party Communism: Parcham and Khalq.* Stanford, CA: Hoover Institution Press, 1983.
Beck, Carl, et al. *Comparative Communist Political Leadership.* New York: David McKay, 1973.
Bialer, Seweryn. "Gorbachev's Program of Change: Sources, Significance, Prospects." *Political Science Quarterly* 103 (Fall 1988): 403-460.
Bialer, Seweryn, and Joan Afferica. "The Genesis of Gorbachev's World." *Foreign Affairs: America and the World 1985* 64, no. 3 (1986): 604-644.
Bialer, Seweryn, and Michael Mendelbaum, eds. *Gorbachev's Russia and American Foreign Policy.* Boulder, CO: Westview Press, 1988.
Blank, Stephen. "Soviet Russia and Low Intensity Conflict in Central Asia: Three Case Studies." In *Low Intensity Conflict in the Third World*,

edited by Lewis Ware et al. Maxwell Air Force Base, AL: Air University Press, 1988.
───. *Stalin's Commissariat of Nationalities: The Sorcerer as Apprentice, 1917-1924.* Dekalb: Northern Illinois University Press, forthcoming.
Brada, Josef. "Soviet Reforms and East European Responses." Paper presented at a conference on New Dimensions of the Polish Economy, October 1987, Wichita, Kansas.
Bradsher, Henry. "Stagnation and Change in Afghanistan." *Journal of South Asian and Middle Eastern Studies* 10 (Fall 1986): 1-35.
Braun, Aurel. "Whither the Warsaw Pact in the Gorbachev Era?" *International Journal* 43 (Winter 1987-88): 63-105.
Brown, Archie. "Gorbachev and Reform of the Soviet System." *Political Quarterly* (April-June 1987): 139-151.
Brown, J. F. "A Western Overview [of the Soviet-U.S. Conference on Eastern Europe]." *Problems of Communism* 37 (May-August 1988): 56-60.
Bunce, Valerie. *Do New Leaders Make a Difference? Executive Succession and Public Policy Under Capitalism and Socialism.* Princeton, NJ: Princeton University Press, 1981.
Chanda, Nayan. "Marriage Made in Moscow." *Far Eastern Economic Review*, June 9, 1988, p. 17.
───. "The New Revolution." *Far Eastern Economic Review*, April 10, 1986, pp. 24-28.
───. "The Sticking Points." *Far Eastern Economic Review*, February 16, 1989, p. 11.
───. "Taking the Soft Line: Vietnam Signals China It Wants Improved Relations." *Far Eastern Economic Review*, December 8, 1988, pp. 27-28.
Clough, Ralph N. *Embattled Korea.* Boulder, CO: Westview Press, 1987.
───. "The Soviet Union and the Two Koreas." In *Soviet Policy in East Asia*, edited by Donald A. Zagoria. New Haven, CT: Yale University Press, 1982.
D'Anastasio, Mark. "Soviets Now Hail China as a Source of Ideas for Reviving Socialism." *Wall Street Journal*, September 18, 1987, p. 1.
Delfs, Robert. "The Sihanouk Card." *Far Eastern Economic Review*, February 11, 1988, p. 35.
"Deng on Sino-Soviet, Sino-American Relations." *Beijing Review*, September 15, 1986, p. 5.
Dobbs, Michael. "A Historic, Tumultuous Summit." *Washington Post National Weekly Edition*, May 22-28, 1989, p. 7.
Duiker, William J. "Vietnam in 1985: Searching for Solutions," *Asian Survey* 26 (January 1986): 102-111.
Ellison, Herbert J. "Changing Sino-Soviet Relations." *Problems of Communism* 36 (May-June 1987): 17-29.
Erlanger, Steven. "Beijing Clarifies Position on Cambodia." *New York Times*, November 14, 1988, p. 3.

Esterline, John H. "Vietnam in 1986: An Uncertain Tiger." *Asian Survey* 27 (January 1987): 92-96.
Fallenbuchl, Zbigniew. "The CMEA and Eastern Europe." *International Journal* 43 (Winter 1987): 106-126.
Fukuyama, Francis. "Gorbachev and the Third World." *Foreign Affairs*, Spring 1986: 715-731.
Galster, Steven. "Rivalry and Reconciliation in Afghanistan: What Prospects for the Accords?" *Third World Quarterly* 10 (October 1988): 1505-1541.
Gargan, Edward A. "China Says Soviets Have a Way To Go." *New York Times*, June 30, 1988, p. 12.
Gati, Charles. "Gorbachev and Eastern Europe." *Foreign Affairs*, Summer 1987: 358-375.
Girardet, Edward. "Russia's War in Afghanistan." *Central Asian Survey* 2, no. 1 (July 1983).
Goldman, Marshall. "Gorbachev's Plan." *New York Times*, August 2, 1987.
Goldman, Marshall, and Merle Goldman. "Soviet and Chinese Economic Reform." *Foreign Affairs* no. 3 (1987-88): 551-573.
Gorbachev, Mikhail. *Perestroika: New Thinking for Our Country and the World*. New York: Harper and Row, 1987.
Gorlin, Alice. "The Soviet Economy." *Current History* 85 (October 1986): 325-328.
Hahn, Werner. "Electoral Choice in the Soviet Bloc." *Problems of Communism* 36 (March-April 1987): 29-39.
Harrison, Selig S. "Containment and the Soviet Union in Afghanistan." In *Containment: Concept and Policy*, edited by Terry L. Deibel and John Lewis Gaddis. Washington, D.C.: National Defense University Press, 1986.
———. "Inside the Afghan Talks." *Foreign Policy* 72 (Fall 1988): 31-60.
Hewitt, Ed A. *Reforming the Soviet Economy: Equality versus Efficiency*. Washington, D.C.: The Brookings Institution, 1988.
Hiebert, Murray. "Carping About Cam Ranh: Hanoi Is Unhappy Over Moscow's Offer on the Base." *Far Eastern Economic Review*, October 27, 1988, p. 27.
Hilsman, Roger. "The Foreign-Policy Consensus: An Interim Research Report." *Journal of Conflict Resolution*, December 1959: 361-382.
Hofheinz, Paul. "Gorbachev's Double Burden: Economic Reform and Growth Acceleration." *Millennium: Journal of International Studies* 16 (Spring 1987): 21-31.
Ignatius, Adi. "Chinese Premier Rules Out Chance of Rapid Reforms." *Wall Street Journal*, April 4, 1989, p. A17.
Indochina Chronology 4, no. 4 (October-December 1985).
Indochina Chronology 5, no. 4 (October-December 1986).
Jones, Ellen, and Benjamin Woodbury. "Chernobyl and Glasnost." *Problems of Communism* 35 (November-December 1986): 28-39.

Judt, Tony. "The Dilemmas of Dissidence: The Politics of Opposition in East-Central Europe." *Eastern European Politics and Society* 2 (Spring 1988).
Kaser, Michael. "One Economy, Two Systems: Parallels Between Soviet and Chinese Reform." *International Affairs* 63 (Summer 1987): 395-412.
Kegley, Charles W., Jr., and Eugene R. Wittkopf. *American Foreign Policy: Pattern and Process*, 3rd ed. New York: St. Martin's Press, 1987.
Keler, Bill. "Gorbachev Praises the Students and Declares Reform Is Necessary." *New York Times*, May 18, 1989, pp. 1, 6.
Kim, Roy. *Soviet-Japanese Relations Under Gorbachev*. Pittsburgh: Russian and East European Study Center, University of Pittsburgh, 1988.
Kimura, Hiroshi. "Soviet Focus on the Pacific." *Problems of Communism* 36 (May-June 1987): 1-15.
Kissinger, Henry. *A World Restored*. Boston: Houghton Mifflin, 1957.
Kuhlman, James A. "A Framework for Viewing Domestic and Foreign Policy Patterns." In *The International Politics of Eastern Europe*, edited by Charles Gati. New York: Praeger Publishers, 1976.
Kundera, Milan. "The Tragedy of Central Europe." *New York Review of Books*, April 26, 1984, pp. 33-38.
Kusin, Vladimir. "What Gorbachev's Reforms Mean for Eastern Europe." Radio Free Europe Research *Background Report* 10 (February 10, 1987).
―――. "Gustav Husak's Strange Absence from the Moscow Parade." Radio Free Europe Research *Background Report* 219 (November 12, 1987).
Lapidus, Gail W. "Gorbachev and the Reform of the Soviet System." *Daedalus* 116 (Spring 1987): 1-30.
Lebahn, Axel. "Political and Economic Effects of Perestroika on the Soviet Union and Its Relations to Eastern Europe and the West." *Aussenpolitik* 39, no. 2 (1988): 107-123.
Levgold, Robert. "The Revolution in Soviet Foreign Policy." *Foreign Affairs, America and the World* 68 (1988-89): 82-98.
Link, Perry. "The Chinese Intellectuals and the Revolt." *New York Review of Books*, June 29, 1989, pp. 38-41.
Lobato, Chantal. "Islam in Kabul: The Religious Politics of Babrak Karmal." *Central Asian Survey* 4, no. 4 (1985): 111-120.
Majrooh, Sayd B. "The Russian Intervention in Afghanistan: The Economic War." *Central Asian Survey* 4, no. 4 (1985): 94-117.
Mason, David, and Dan Nelson. "Political Apathy in Poland." *Studium Papers* 12 (July 1988): 68-81.
McCauley, Martin, and Stephen Carter, eds. *Leadership and Succession in the Soviet Union, Eastern Europe and China*. Armonk, NY: M. E. Sharpe, 1986.
McGregor, Charles. "The Sino-Vietnamese Relationship and the Soviet Union." *Adelphi Papers*, no. 232 (Autumn 1988).

Mesa-Lago, Carmelo. "The Cuban Economy in the 1980s: The Return of Ideology." In *Socialist Cuba, Past Interpretations and Future Challenges*, edited by Sergio Roca. Boulder, CO: Westview Press, 1988.

Nations, Richard. "Great Leap Sideways." *Far Eastern Economic Review*, May 30, 1985, pp. 15-16.

———. "Moscow's New Tack." *Far Eastern Economic Review* August 14, 1986, pp. 30-34.

Newman, Joseph Jr. "The Future of Northern Afghanistan." *Asian Survey* 38 (July 1988): 729-739.

Noorzoy, M. Siddieq. "Long-Term Soviet Economic Interests and Policies in Afghanistan." In *Afghanistan: The Great Game Revisited*, edited by Roseanne Klass. New York: Freedom House, 1987.

Perez-Lopez, Jorge F. "Cuban Hard-Currency Trade and Oil Reexports." In *Socialist Cuba, Past Interpretations and Future Challenges*, edited by Sergio Roca. Boulder, CO: Westview Press, 1988.

Petrov, Vladimir. "Gorbachev Looks at Asia." *Journal of Northeast Asian Studies* 4 (Winter 1985): 26-44.

Pike, Douglas. *Vietnam and the Soviet Union: Anatomy of an Alliance.* Boulder, CO: Westview Press, 1987.

Pravda, Alex. "In the Eastern Bloc." *Los Angeles Times*, August 23, 1988.

Quinn-Judge, Paul. "Return to Moscow." *Far Eastern Economic Review*, August 2, 1984, pp. 24-26.

Quinn-Judge, Sophie, and Murray Hiebert. "Ten Year Itch: Soviets Admit Much of Economic Aid to Hanoi Was Wasted." *Far Eastern Economic Review*, November 10, 1988, p. 23.

Robertson, Myles L. C. *Soviet Policy Towards Japan: An Analysis of Trends in the 1970s and 1980s.* Cambridge: Cambridge University Press, 1988.

Rozman, Gilbert. "China's Soviet Watchers in the 1980s: A New Era of Scholarship." *World Politics* 37 (July 1985): 435-474.

———. *The Chinese Debate About Soviet Socialism, 1978-1985.* Princeton, NJ: Princeton University Press, 1987.

Rubinstein, Alvin Z. ed. *Soviet and Chinese Influence in the Third World.* New York: Praeger Publishers, 1975.

Segal, Gerald. "The USSR and Asia in 1987: Sign of a Major Effort." *Asian Survey* 28, no. 1 (January 1988): 1-9.

Sestanovich, Stephen. "Gorbachev's Foreign Policy: A Diplomacy of Decline." *Problems of Communism* 37 (January-February 1988): 1-15.

Shahrani, M. Nazif, and Robert Canfield, eds. *Revolutions and Rebellions in Afghanistan: Anthropological Perspectives.* Berkeley: Institute of International Studies, University of California, 1984.

Shroder, John F., and Abdul Tawab Assifi. "Afghan Mineral Resources and Soviet Exploration." In *Afghanistan: The Great Game Revisited*, edited by Roseanne Klass. New York: Freedom House, 1987.

Silver, Brian. "Political Beliefs of the Soviet Citizen." In *Politics, Work, and Daily Life in the USSR*, edited by James Millar. Cambridge: Cambridge University Press, 1987.

Starr, S. Frederick. "Soviet Union: A Civil Society." *Foreign Policy* no. 70 (Spring 1988): 26-41.

Strode, Dan L. "Soviet China Policy in Flux." *Survival* 30 (July/August 1988): 339-340.

Su, Chi. "China and the Soviet Union: 'Principled, Salutary and Tempered' Management of Conflict." In *China and the World*, edited by Samuel S. Kim. Boulder, CO: Westview Press, 1984.

Swing, John Temple. "Afghanistan After the Accords: A Report from Kabul." *Critical Issues* (Council on Foreign Relations) 6 (1988).

Tyson, Ann Scott. "Sino-Soviet Talks Mark 'Common Ground' on Cambodia Conflict." *Christian Science Monitor*, September 2, 1988, p. 7.

Uhlig, Mark. "Prague Waits for a Thaw." *New York Times Magazine*, September 4, 1988.

Urban, Joan Barth. "Gorbachev and the Communist World: Collapse or Perestroika?" *Problems of Communism* 37 (September-October 1988): 71-76.

U.S. Department of State, Bureau of Intelligence and Research. "Afghanistan and Soviet Nationalities." In *Soviet Nationalities Survey* 14. Washington, D.C.: Government Printing Office, March 1, 1988.

U.S. Department of State, Bureau of Public Affairs. "Human Rights in Cuba: An Update." Washington, D.C.: Government Printing Office, January 1989.

White, Stephen. "Economic Performance and Communist Legitimacy." *World Politics* 3 (April 1986): 462-482.

World Military Expenditures and Arms Transfers, 1987. Washington, D.C.: U.S. Arms Control and Disarmament Agency, 1988.

Index

Afanasyev, Victor, 47
Afghanistan, Democratic Republic of, 112, 118, 158-159; effects of war, 119-120
Afghanistan, People's Democratic Party of, 109-110; Balkanization of, 118-123
Amnesty International, 75

Brezhnev, Leonid, 42-43
Brezhnev Doctrine, 3, 27, 34, 155

Cambodia, 5, 99, 100-101
Campaign of Rectification of Errors (Cuba), 68, 69, 71
Castro, Fidel, 66, 67, 74, 155; commitment to socialism, 66-67; human rights, 74-76; perception of socialism, 68-69, 70, 73, 78; perestroika, 70-71, 155
Chernobyl, 7
Children of the Arbat (Rybakov), 7, 17
China, People's Republic of, 41; agricultural policy, 52; democracy movement (May-June 1988), 47; economic reforms, 45; economic ties with the Soviet Union, 49-51; foreign trade, 42; reaction to perestroika, 45-47, 57-58; special economic zones, 52
Congress of People's Deputies (Soviet Union), 7
Council for Mutual Economic Assistance, 12, 119
Cuba, 63ff., 83-84; intelligentsia, 83; mass media, 83; National Assembly, 72, 80; reaction to perestroika, 155; reform, 68
Cuban Committee for Human Rights, 74, 76-77
Cuban Communist Party, 70, 71-72
Czechoslovakia, 3; dissent, 31-32, 158; economic reforms, 3, 29-30; reaction to perestroika, 27-28, 155

Deng Xiaoping, 41-42, 48, 54, 91
Dr. Zhivago (Pasternak), 7, 19
Dubcek, Alexander, 31, 32

Eastern Europe: economic growth, 12; obstacles to reform, 35-36; relations with Soviet Union, 1-2, 11-15, 35, 154

elites, 64, 159
Estonia, 1, 9

Fojtik, Jan, 30-31

Gati, Charles, 14
General Agreement on Tariffs and Trade, 12
Ghulabzoi, Sayed M., 117, 123
glasnost: causes, 4-5; 162-163; defined, 5, 6, 63
Glasnost, 8
Gorbachev, Mikhail, 3, 5, 8-9, 63-71, 90, 147, 160-161, 162; on Brezhnev Doctrine, 34; Bucharest speech, 12-13; on China, 44, 54; on Czechoslovakia, 14; on Eastern Europe, 12-13; interest in Poland, 22-24, 26; Krasnoyarsk speech, 136; need to reform, 131, 139; on religion, 8; on Rumania, 14; UN speech, 10; view of Yugoslavia, 12-13; visit to Cuba, 78-82; visit to Cuba, assessment, 82; visit to Poland, 24-25; Vladivostok speech, 98-99, 130, 134, 139

Hilsman, Roger, 152
Ho Chi Minh, 88-89
Hoc Tap (Vietnam), 88
Hungary, 1; 1956 revolt, 15
Husak, Gustav, 3, 15, 28

Izvestia, 25

Jakes, Milos, 3, 28-29
jamming: by Czechoslovakia, 31; by Poland, 19; by Soviet Union, 7
Jaruzelski, Wojciech, 17, 18, 20, 23

Kadar, Janos, 14-15
Karmal, Babrak, 109-110, 114
Katyn Forest, 20-21, 27

Khazakhstan, 8
Kim Il Sung, 138-139
Kiszczak, Czeslaw, 22, 25
Kommunist, 9, 18, 48
Korea, People's Republic of, 138, 140; relations with Republic of Korea, 141-142; view of perestroika, 140-141
Korea, Republic of, 141-142; economic development, 132-133; multinational corporations, 134; relations with People's Republic of Korea, 140-141; trade with Soviet Union, 135; U.S. forces, 142
Kuhlman, James, 152-153, 157, 159
Kulerski, Wiktor, 22
Kuron, Jacek, 9

Law on State Enterprises (Soviet Union), 5
Le Duan, 90, 92, 93
Le Duc Tro, 92, 93
Ligachev, Igor, 94
Li Peng, 47, 91
Literaturnaya Gazieta, 21

Marxism-Leninism in Cuba, 64-66, 70-71, 76, 78; in Korea, 140
Messner, Prime Minister, 23, 25
Michnik, Adam, 19-20, 34
Miodowicz, Alfred, 25
Moscow News, 4, 33, 52
Mujaheddin, 113

Nabokov, Vladimir, 7
Najibullah, President, 110-117
new thinking, 9-11, 53, 63, 98; impact on Vietnam, 103-105
Nguyen Van Linh, 95-96, 97-102
nomenklatura, 6, 8

Pacific Economic Cooperation Conference, 134

Pak Dong-jin, 134-135
Pasternak, Boris, 7
perestroika, 6, 131, 162-163; causes, 4-5; defined, 5, 63; perceptions, China, 45-47, 57-58; perceptions, Cuba, 70-71; perceptions, Korea, 140-141
Perestroika (Gorbachev), 139-140
Pham Van Dong, 91, 92, 93
Poland, 1, 2-3, 158; censorship, 19; debt, 21; history of reforms, 16-27; interest in Soviet reforms, 17, 161; public views of socialism, 22, 155
Polish United Workers' Party, 26, 158
Polityka, 17, 19
Prague Spring, 3, 27-28, 32-33; Soviet evaluation, 33
Pravda, 9, 10, 24-25, 27, 44, 48
Primakov, Yevgeniy, 10, 24-25, 134

Rakowski, Mieczyslaw, 23
Reagan, Ronald, 91; administration, 144
Rogachev, Igor, 102-103, 138
Roh Tae Woo, 129, 131, 132-133, 136, 143
Rozman, Gilbert, 42
Russian Orthodox Church, 8
Rybakov, Anatoly, 7, 17

Sabata, Jaroslav, 32
Sakharov, Andrei, 1, 8, 16
Seoul Olympics, 130, 143
Shanghai Communiqué, 53
Sharq, Hassan, 115-116
Shevardnadze, Eduard, 10, 54, 95, 103, 118
Sihanouk, Norodom, 56, 101
socialism: Cuban, 68-69, 70, 73, 78; in Poland, 22, 155
socialist community, 151-152, 162

Solidarity, 15-16, 19, 22, 26, 158
Soviet National Committee for Asia Pacific Economic Cooperation, 134
Soviet Union: aid to Cuba, 81; aid to Vietnam, 94; analysis of Chinese reforms, 51-52, 57; and Cambodia, 100-101; domestic reform, 4-9, 13, 131; and Eastern Europe, 5-6, 11-15, 102, 154; economic ties with China, 49-51; and Poland, 15-27; policy toward Afghanistan, 114, 118-119, 121; policy toward Cuba, 160; policy toward religion, 8; policy toward Vietnam, 87-104; trade with Republic of Korea, 135
System of Economic Management and Planning (Cuba), 66, 69

Time, 30
Truong Chinh, 92, 93

United Nations Human Rights Commission, 75
uskorienie (acceleration), 5, 131

Vietnam, Communist Party of, 90, 92ff, 158
Vietnam, Socialist Republic of, 87ff., 158; aid from Soviet Union, 94; economic reforms, 96-97; policy toward Cambodia, 102; policy toward Soviet Union, 87-104
Voice of America, 79-80

Walesa, Lech, 20, 22-23, 26

Yagodovsky, Leonid, 33

Zahir Shah, King, 115, 124
Zaslavskaya, Tatyana, 6-7, 9

About the Editors and Contributors

CHARLES BUKOWSKI is an Assistant Professor with the Institute of International Studies at Bradley University, Peoria, Illinois. His most recent research focuses on public policy in Eastern Europe and Yugoslav politics. He was coeditor (with Mark A. Cichock, 1987) of *Prospects for Change in Socialist Systems.* His previous work has appeared in *Coexistence* and *Eastern European Politics and Societies.*

J. RICHARD WALSH is an Assistant Professor of Political Science at Wittenberg University, Springfield, Ohio. He is the author of *Change, Continuity and Commitment: China's Adaptive Foreign Policy* (1988) and has published articles on Chinese reforms and Sino-American relations in *Asian Affairs* and *The Journal of Northeast Asian Studies.* In 1987-88 he was the Visiting Professor of Asian Studies, U.S. Air War College, Maxwell AFB, Alabama.

STEPHEN BLANK is Associate Professor of Soviet Studies at the Center for Aerospace Doctrine, Research and Education, Maxwell AFB, Alabama. He is the author of the forthcoming *Stalin's Commissariat of Nationalities: The Sorcerer as Apprentice, 1917-1924.* He has published many articles on Soviet nationality policies, foreign policies in the Muslim Third World, and the war in Afghanistan. He has also taught at the University of Texas at San Antonio and the University of California, at Riverside.

JUAN M. del AGUILA is an Associate Professor of Political Science and Director of the Center for International Studies at Emory University, Atlanta. Some of his previous work has appeared in *Inter-American Studies*, *Current History*, and *World Affairs*. He has contributed several chapters to books and is the author of *Cuba: Dilemmas of a Revolution* (1988).

ROY U.T. KIM is a Professor of Political Science at Drexel University, Philadelphia. He has published several articles on Korean affairs and is a frequent commentator on current events in the region. One of his most recent publications is *Soviet-Japanese Relations Under Gorbachev* (1988).

DAVID S. MASON is Associate Professor of Political Science at Butler University, Indianapolis. He has published widely on Polish politics, East European politics, and Soviet-East European relations, including articles in *Slavic Review*, *Journal of Politics*, *Current History*, and *International Affairs*. His book, *Public Opinion and Political Change in Poland* was published in 1985. He was a Hoover Institution Fellow in 1989 and is currently working on an international collaborative project entitled "Perceptions of Justice in East and West."

DANIEL S. PAPP is Professor of International Affairs and Director of the School of Social Sciences at Georgia Institute of Technology, Atlanta. He has written several articles and chapters and edited books on Soviet security policy and policy toward the Third World. Recent publications include *Soviet Perceptions of the Developing World in the 1980s: The Ideological Basis* (1985) and *Contemporary International Relations: Frameworks for Understanding* (1988).